INKLINGS

INKLINGS

A Meditative Memoir

Evelyn J. Bergstrom

Art by Pat Van de Graaf

Copyright © 2005 by Evelyn J. Bergstrom.

Art by Pat Van de Graaf

Library of Congress Number: 2004099831
ISBN: Hardcover 1-4134-7134-X
Softcover 1-4134-7133-1

All rights reserved. No part of this book may be reproduced or transmitted in any form or by any means, electronic or mechanical, including photocopying, recording, or by any information storage and retrieval system, without permission in writing from the copyright owner.

This book was printed in the United States of America.

To order additional copies of this book, contact:
Xlibris Corporation
1-888-795-4274
www.Xlibris.com
Orders@Xlibris.com

26728

Need knocked on the door of my soul,
and I finally responded.
It's the season, I said, to be fruitful.
And God said, in due season, you will be.

'Tis the season.
Thanks be to God.

This book is dedicated to
the God I know in Jesus Christ
and
my beloved husband and best friend, Bob.

With grateful acknowledgment for the loving support
of all my friends and family who encouraged this endeavor,
and with special thanks to my artist friend Pat,
whose images
so beautifully enhance my words.

CONTENTS

Whisperings

The Word whispers to us
When we walk or when we lay;
It is only our inner clamor
That keeps us away
From the prayer that our heart
Lifts up. Each day.

The Word whispers to us
And we turn a deaf ear,
Distracted from the very message
That we need to hear
To transform our being—
Word by word, year by year.

Attend those whispers of the Word
That rustle in your heart.
Still yourself. Put aside all else,
Let your thoughts not dart
To silence the gift
That God would impart.

Hear the whispers of the Word.

IN
BEGINNING
WAS THE
WORD

IN THE BEGINNING . . .

Beginning to share with others the private whispers of God's word is both scary and difficult. But I take heart from the opening of John's gospel: "In the beginning was the Word, and the Word was with God, and the Word was God." For today I would begin the daunting task of writing about "the word" as it came to me, personally and potently: *the* word, always one particular word, given to me like a unique benediction, presented one word at a time in my daily meditation over a spiritually rich period of several months.

At that particular time, in the midst of my long-established daily meditation practice, when I entered a certain stage of receptivity, I began to be "given" a word that peculiarly demanded my exclusive attention. Suddenly and unexpectedly a common word vested with mysterious awesomeness would arise from a creative source, the Other. My consciousness would abruptly dam up mid-stream, stranding all other thoughts and eddying around just one word. It was impossible to flow forward, to ignore this powerful frisson of intuitive recognition, this clear summons to devote my entire attention to this one word, which stood solidly planted like an immovable rock.

The experience was not unlike the practice of *lectio divina*, a slow and meditative reading of scripture to search for words that "shimmer" or beckon the reader to follow them into pathways of more focused application for the here-and-now of life. A practitioner of *lectio divina* chooses to concentrate on mining the selected verses of scripture for deeper levels of meaning and personal significance. The starting point of meditation is always the Bible.

My experience felt akin to *lectio divina* but with one singular exception: it was unmediated by scripture. In my meditation I seemed to be responding to a direct inspiration of the Spirit, then taken by the hand and led into the presence of God: the *word* chose *me*.

And it felt like such a *living* word, a visual STOP sign, a blessing brought into the shore of my soul by a wave of God's grace.

Since my own initiation into this phenomenon, I have read that the poet Rilke felt that he had received what he termed "inner dictations," words given to him with the same persistence and urgency I had experienced. In prayerful times I believe our Creator communicates to us through those windows to the sacred, imagination and fantasy—and we are apt to take the credit rather than attribute it to the Source.

As this "word-giving" phenomenon persisted, I came to treasure each word as a special gift from God. No matter how strange or incomprehensible the given word would appear to be, each had all the hallmarks of the gift of the Spirit: each was surprising and unexpected, insistent and compelling, accompanied by the feeling of awe and mystery, potent and commanding, out-of-the-ordinary and pregnant with possibility.

Pregnant with possibility . . . but still unbirthed. A divine gift, but still "unwrapped." Insight would come only upon reflection, with journaling to illumine the significance of the word to me, and with follow-up research in dictionaries, etymological sources and scriptural references. Slowly, slowly do we come to understanding, even when so personally addressed by God. A gift can easily remain "under wraps," hidden from the eyes of the heart, unconverted to wisdom. Reflection is what separates the flash-in-the-pan moment from the true Light, what enfleshes word as the Living Word.

In the words of Macrina Wiederkehr, from her book, *Song of the Seed*: "God's call unfolds, a word at a time, slowly." Slowly, as life itself unfolds, do we realize all that God would communicate to us. Slowly do we develop a heightened awareness to hear and respond to Divine prompts.

In prayer I stand on the threshold and seek the doorway into my soul, God's own sanctuary. In this mystical "thin place" (so named by the Celtic tradition) some inklings from the great beyond occasionally break through. The stillness sought in contemplative prayer encourages these inklings, mere hints and suggestions of "something more" than is visible during the daily welter of confusing demands, to penetrate chinks in the walls of our psyche. An inkling can provide a peephole into God's realm of truth; with further reflection, the pray-er can harvest insights of transformative power.

Now, years later after the experience of receiving each of these special words, there is time to reflect even more deeply on each one of them, to discern what God was communicating through the medium of one word at a time. And I would be *obedient*, true to the original meaning of that word, which means to listen deeply and attentively, to be "all ears" for God, to let God's word seep into my center and percolate, and then to grow and share the fruits of the Spirit with others.

It is probably no coincidence that, as I resolved to write these essays, I began my quiet time of prayer this morning with Psalm 103, and verse 20 spoke to me:

Bless the Lord, you angels of his,
you mighty ones who do his bidding,
and hearken to the voice of his word.

In this small work I would "hearken" to this voice, which speaks to us persistently if we but listen, perhaps bestowing upon us only one word at a time in a still, small voice.

And so I begin at the beginning, with the first word ever so received as the first chapter of this book. I invite you to ponder along with me, to accompany me as I reveal how the word unfolded in my journaling . . . and to search for your own meanings in these words, for they are gifts to me and to you.

PAT
WATCH

ON BEING ALERT

It came like a thunderbolt in the midst of my morning meditation: an ordinary word infused with extraordinary power. Out of a storm of thoughts, the simple word *watch* demanded all my attention.

Watch, I thought, watch *what*? And then, a train of other questions roared through my mind. Watch *for* what? *Why* watch, and *when* and *how*? Could this be a summons (it felt so imperative!) to be on the lookout for the unexpected, to become more observant as I pace through my daily routines? Do I need to look beyond the obvious, to hone my skills of observation to penetrate the hiddenness in relationships? Is God calling me by a special message, this gift of the word *watch*, to a heightened sense of awareness of myself and others and this world we share?

Many questions, no immediate answers. But my primary gut reaction was that I couldn't ignore such a compelling one-word command. Although totally unsure that any firm answers would result, I was certain that I must struggle to decode this single-word message for my own spiritual wholeness.

When I ran out of my own top-of-the-head associations, I sought out the etymological dictionary as a resource for further illumination. There I found that in ancient times "watch" had a clear connection with "wake," for both words share the common Anglo-Saxon root *wacian*. No wonder *watch* seemed to be such a magnetic word for me—it was a wake-up call!

Originally watch was associated only with nighttime, and the old expression "watch and ward" was meant to cover both night (watch) and day (ward). What really surprised me was to discover that a "watch meeting" was equivalent to our New Year's Eve, and the "watch-night service" describes the old custom of ushering in the new year by attending a religious meeting on the night of December 31. Could it be a new *watch*word for me—the rallying cry to wake up to a new season of renewal and spiritual growth?

Maybe in God's view it's less important for us to see with clarity than to be faithful over time on our watch: God may just value the process more than the end result. Typically, watches are vigils that take place in the dark, where seeing clearly is not a possibility. In the dark our eyes fail, but we call on our other senses to become more acute; we escalate the efforts of our whole self to be vigilant in order to apprehend what is happening by whatever means we can. Most especially we develop a keen ability to listen. Could God be urging me to new depths of listening in both prayer and my relationships?

By nature I have always been more comfortable as an observer of others rather than a person who enjoys being center stage myself. So I truly felt that I was *already* watching more than most people. Why then had I received this clear but mysterious call to *watch*? As I searched my memory to recall the word *watch* in scripture, the first verses that popped up came from Psalm 130:

I wait for the Lord, my soul waits,
And in his word I hope;
My soul waits for the Lord

more than the watchmen for the morning
more than the watchmen for the morning.

So *watch* is connected with waiting, I thought. That makes sense.

. . . Waiting in the dark for morning, the light, to come.

. . . Waiting for the dawn of a new day.

Waiting can be a time of pregnant expectation, a vigil that demands our acute attention. Waiting is the theme that begins the Christian church year in the season of Advent as we wait for the miracle of the Christ child come to earth—Emmanuel, God with us. Anticipating once again the birth of Jesus, these twenty centuries later. And what do we do while we wait? We prepare: we set a watch on our own inner spirit, put ourselves on notice to examine our foibles and aim God's light into the shadows of our own hearts. We aim to create sacred space for the very spirit of Christ to be born anew in us.

That's an elevated, spiritual view of waiting, however. In our practical everyday world, waiting is not a revered pastime. In fact, most people equate waiting with doing absolutely nothing, suffering through a time of boredom and inactivity. It conjures up images of toe-tapping, finger-drumming impatience. A monumental waste of time. But we do not have to accede to this popular image of waiting as a time of frustration. Waiting is an "in-between" time, the space caught up in the midst of what has already happened and what will or might happen, a time of transition. How far we adults stray from childhood, to prefer the surety of knowing rather than the anticipation of the unknown! Waiting is neither before nor after: it is the present. The challenge is to use the present well as we wait . . . and watch.

Long ago I decided that waiting on lines, waiting for others, waiting for happenings could be a time of watchfulness—not dispassionate observation, but caring watchfulness. Those people with whom I am waiting, or for whom I am waiting, need my prayers. Inside they carry untold stories of sorrow, disappointment, dashed hopes and dreams, and also joyous tales of love and achievement. If I endeavor to "see" them in a different way—with eyes of love instead of judgment—then I cease to be an empty observer who is using eyes only to watch the passing scene. Love gives me the vision of the heart.

And often, surprisingly, those I watch turn to me. My very aura of quiet watchfulness seems to draw people into my circle of caring. Others sense that I have inner space available for them, that I will listen. And finding a good listener is a rare commodity in our too-frantic world. So, in my experience, frequently those I have been watching draw close and begin to divulge their deeper selves; at times I am completely surprised by the intimate details of life that even strangers are willing and eager to share. So deep is their desire to be heard that any ear will do, and any commentary required is usually minimal. And I continue to watch as they speak, noting their body language and the expressions that accompany their words. These subliminal messages often send the most powerful signals of their inner feelings to a caring listener.

But I confess that I am not always so watchful, so alive in the Spirit. Sometimes I fail miserably to watch with eyes of love, and then I feel a humble camaraderie with the disciples who succumbed to sleep in the garden of Gethsemane; Jesus had directly asked them to watch with him, but they could not stay awake. When my own spirit bows to weariness, then indifference supplants watchfulness and I allow a spiritual torpor to overcome my best caring self. Others around me are almost immediately aware that I have "neutralized" myself by means of detachment. Perhaps I have become supersaturated with suffering images: all those homeless, hungry people in the streets, all those refugees stranded by war outside their homelands, all the angry gestures and strident voices of opposing political views. Who can bear these sights without reaching one's personal limit of compassion? At those times I consciously turn away from watching; I defend myself from the pain of others' sufferings.

It is not humanly possible to sustain a caring watchfulness without God as our companion. We wear down and burn out when we depend solely on our own resources. This human predilection is recognized by St. Benedict in his Rule. He says: "Hour by hour keep careful watch over all you do, aware that God's gaze is upon you, wherever you may be" (4.48-9). Now I don't interpret this Rule as portraying God as "Big Brother," ready to pounce on us so we had better be good! No, instead I feel accompanied by a watchful and merciful companion, One who encourages me to expand my perceptions, to cultivate a spiritual vision in the midst of mundane happenings, to watch and evaluate all that I'm about, to be careful of how I spend my hours. It echoes Psalm 141:3:

Set a watch before my mouth, O Lord,
and guard the door of my lips;
let not my heart incline to any evil thing.

The willingness to be receptive to God's watchfulness, and to allow God to increase our own watchfulness, is cultivated time after time in our own prayer and meditation moments. My daily prayer time, set aside early in the morning, is perhaps an unconscious response to Psalm 5:3:

In the morning, Lord, you hear my voice;
early in the morning I make my appeal and watch for you.

As we clear out and make space for God, we place ourselves on watch for God's spirit moving through our lives. In our prayerful vigil we seek surprises and revelations; perhaps there will be new pathways over unfamiliar territory, or old pathways that reveal previously undiscovered treasures. But we must be awake, alive to the moment, because a sleepwalker will not be prepared to receive the blessings God wants to bestow as a gift. As a verse from Proverbs instructs us (4:23):

More than all else,
keep watch over your heart,
since here are the wellsprings of life.

The very next morning after *watch* surprised me during my meditation, I was startled to discover my newly-revealed word in a line of an old standard hymn, *The Church's One Foundation*. It felt like a totally new thought to sing "The saints their *watch* are keeping," followed by the most plaintive of all questions: "how long?" In my mind I answered, "All life long, I guess, for those who begin the quest of a spiritual journey." We have to keep on keeping on—our watch is never over.

What's in a small five-letter word? Everything! If God ponders it with you . . . or you ponder it with God.

PAT

IS GOD A MASTER MUSICIAN?

Harmony—that was the second word, given during meditation in the same awesome way as I received the first. Initially being called to *watch*, that state of wakeful alertness of all my senses; now a shift of focus, a call to concentrate on hearing, especially seeking the sounds of *harmony*.

What could this new word be saying to me? Personally, the word *harmony* evokes a stream of questions. What do I need to bring into harmony in my own life? Exactly what would my experience be like, and feel like, if the strands of my life were blended in harmony? How do I promote harmony in my relationships? Where do I see evidence of harmony, and where do I hear discord, in my own life circles and the greater world?

Despite my questions, for the most part *harmony* was certainly comforting to think about—it's a "feel-good" word, altogether pleasant, evoking a sense of well-being that "all's right with the world." When life is harmonious, the various pieces of the day seem to fit together well, if not perfectly. For the inner life this brings a certain feeling of peace and contentment; in relationships between people, harmony means a certain consonance, with no large issues or disagreements to cause people to act at odds with one another. No bad vibrations with harmony, only pleasing synonyms: concord, peace, unity, amity, friendship—and, of course, in music, harmony means a wonderful blend of simultaneous tones pleasing to our ears.

Recently a headline over a letter in the N.Y. Times caught my eye: "Music as Ultimate Reality." It drew attention to a letter from Joseph Eger, the conductor of the U.N. Symphony, who exuberantly declared: "I postulate that the universe, macro and micro, is made of music!"

Maybe Mr. Eger is on to something here, I thought. His statement began a chain-reaction in my mind: at its essence, music is sound waves, vibrations and energy; these sound waves, each one a singular element, are the stuff of musical composition, capable of being used in an infinite variety of sequences to create an infinite number of melodies and harmonies—or disharmonies.

Out of this bevy of vibrational possibilities, a musical composer creates a sequence of notes, imposing order by his choices and juxtapositions. And this we call music, the art of sound in time, acknowledged as the universal language. Without the composer's intention and intervention, those sound vibrations can just result in noise, not music. It is the composer's search for complementary tones that results in harmony.

Music not only engenders harmony but it enables us to reach far beyond the layers of rational thought; music crashes through any protective guards we've set up at the doorway to our soul, right to our deep heart. As eloquently stated by Herbert Spencer, the British philosopher and sociologist, "Music must take rank as the highest of the fine arts—as the one which, more than any other, ministers to human welfare."

In a later article in the Science section of the N.Y. Times (4/4/2000), some scientists underscored Conductor Eger's intuition by declaring that the superstring theory is the pathway to understanding the universe. These scientists perceive the universe as "kind of mathematical music played by an orchestra of tiny vibrating strings. Each note in this cosmic symphony would represent one of the many different kinds of particles that make up matter and energy." Physicist Brian Greene, author of *The Elegant Universe,* writes that "musical metaphors take on a startling reality, for the [superstring] theory suggests that the microscopic landscape is suffused with tiny strings whose vibrational patterns orchestrate the evolution of the cosmos."

Amazing—musicians and physicists agree! Maybe God *is* a Master Musician giving us wonderful harmonies to hear when we are still, and hoping to have us respond harmoniously. Maybe music *is* very near to the Ultimate Reality, the heart of God.

Harmony is but one element of music. It joins with rhythm ("the beat"), time (the cadence) and melody (the recognizable song line) to augment and enhance the sounds. The resulting music has the power to still our incessant inner dialogue; we quiet ourselves to listen deeply to the blending of the voices or instruments, the various intonations, the pattern of the composition. We feel in the grasp of "something greater" than ourselves. We listen with awe to the incredible interplay of tones, to the musicians using all their expertise to hit the exact notes, to the unity and integrity of the orchestra or chorus, where many persons and/or instruments are united in a common purpose, to create a memorable and beautiful sound.

I remember clearly my first conscious inkling of the power and beauty of music. Like all important memories, it is etched in my brain and psyche: the time, the place, the age, the circumstance. I was nine years old, in the fourth grade of

Haledon Grammar School, on Kossuth Street in Haledon, New Jersey. Our teacher, Mrs. Taggi, introduced us to Edward Grieg's "Peer Gynt Suite": the rollicking "In the Hall of the Mountain King," the mournful "Asa's Death," and the lyrical "Anitra's Dance." Never before had I heard music telling a story—it was a magical moment. And even today I cannot hear "Peer Gynt" without being transported back to that classroom, its smells and sounds, and all my childhood friends. Musical associations evoke memories and touch our emotions like no other artistic creation.

Over the years my love of music, especially classical music, has deepened. Joy is listening to my favorite CDs or WQXR, New York City's classical music station. Unfortunately, I am only an appreciator, not a creator of music. Although I love music, all kinds of music, I am completely unschooled in any aspect of it. I neither play an instrument nor sing—unlike many choir members, I cannot consider my voice an instrument that makes harmonious sounds! Yet in my depths I know there is music, for I have been surprised at its welling up, and though I cannot reproduce the melodies for others, I can "hear" this inner music in all its power and loveliness.

Let me share some special moments I have had with such music upwelling inside. The first time this ever happened was during a silent retreat, a weekend at a monastery. In the atmosphere of that holy place of silence, my inner world eventually became very still; I had countless hours to write in my journal and to "empty out." Suddenly and unexpectedly during one of my meditations, snatches of music rose up within me, from the center of the stillpoint I had reached. I recognized themes from congregational hymns that I had sung (in my own inimitable style!) and from choir anthems that I could never hope to sing. Evoked by my innermost thoughts and emotions, the music was expressing the inexpressible for me. Beyond words.

My insight: when deep silence is reached, there is music. The muse of meditation, Melete, is not ever far from her sister Aoede, the muse of song. Deep within, where God is, there is a place that is singing.

If we take the instruments of the orchestra, and think of them as separate persons, with particular talents and abilities, we see that each plays a special part, giving forth a distinctive tone that contributes to the richness and depth of life's music. Each instrument produces its unique sound and stays true to the range it can perform: the flute does not try to emulate the horn, the trumpet does not strive to be a violin. Individually, the instruments of the orchestra "stay in character" and each exhibits an unswerving commitment to play its part well, and the synergy of the overall blended sound not only is inspiring but is a marvel to our ears.

St. Paul urges us in Colossians 3:13:

> *And above all these put on love,*
> *which binds everything together in perfect harmony.*

Isn't being *in tune* with God or others just another way of saying that we have "put on love"? In those rare moments when we have tuned in, paid attention, listened closely, we realize we have discovered that elusive gift: *harmony*, a peace of spirit both within ourselves and between ourselves and others. God set the tone and we just "tuned in" to God's wavelength. The secret of the spiritual life may hinge on being an "in tune" instrument that God can play!

Harmony seems to result when we clothe ourselves with the love Paul espouses, love that elicits from us our best strains of compassion, kindness, humility, patience, faithfulness and forgiveness. We have a choice: we can be tone-deaf, choosing to be a "noisy gong or a clanging cymbal" (1 Cor.13: 1), or we can "put on love" so we can play our part with balance, dedication, commitment and joy.

PAT

DOWN WITH NOISE!

Do you snorkel? Those who do know that there's a special meditative quality about snorkeling: you become very aware of your breathing, you cannot speak, you are cradled by the water and immersed in something much bigger than yourself. It all adds up to a mesmerizing experience, as you witness the wonders of the sea from a new perspective. What was hidden from the shore is revealed in the depths.

Contemplation in the presence of God has many of these same attributes: you certainly pay close attention to your breathing, you seek to communicate beyond words, you literally swim in the Spirit as you clear your mind and dwell with God. And you emerge from this sea of the Spirit refreshed and renewed, knowing that the very stillness has nourished you.

The familiar "Be still and know that I am God" from Psalm 46 has always spoken to me; my guess is that we appropriate biblical verses that are essential to our own spiritual condition. Certainly I *know* I must seek to be still in prayer, to create space for God's voice to emerge within what otherwise is my ongoing monologue. But I need scripture as a reminder: seeking that stillpoint is an elusive target for me. Then came the word given one morning: *still.* And I followed God's lead to ruminate on this word.

How challenging it is to still our thoughts! The norm for most of us is an internal running monologue: incessant considerations of our own personal agenda, with an array of anxieties and decisions vying for clarity and resolution. Our circuitous thought-loops are as endless as a NASCAR race . . . and as noisy!

It's easier by far to relax into snorkeling than to clear our minds for contemplation, a serious discipline that demands utmost focus and attention. Being still is creating spiritual space, be that for others or the Other. It requires that we stop our babbling minds to step into the still waters of Psalm 23, where there is respite from our teeming thoughts and refreshment for our spirit. At the heart of stillness God stands ready to slake our thirst.

One of my favorite places of stillness is a pond within walking distance of my home. There I can rest on my "meditation rock" and contemplate the beauty of the trees and sky reflected on the water's surface. To be truthful, nothing much happens. Birds twitter, hawks soar, and sometimes deer and ducks visit. An occasional turtle floats up from the depths to gulp some air. But mostly the pond is an oasis of unbroken quiet that elicits a response:

Gratefully, my spirit turns to You,
Seeking your presence by the waterside;
Grace pours down and renews.
Fragile, my thoughts find expression,
Coming forth on wobbly legs
Like a toddling child.
Go to your pond,
Distilling reflections from the depths;
It will teach you all.

Unfortunately, not every visit to my pond sanctuary calms my spirit. At times its usual peacefulness has been disrupted and I have turned toward home with a rueful smile and unfulfilled expectations. Nevertheless, through disappointment I gained a fresh perspective:

O God, I seek the stillness of my pond sanctuary;
And instead of a soothing, murmuring brook
I find a pair of noisy geese—
What an object lesson!
How often my mind squawks with noisy demands
Even when I purposely come to be quiet
In your Presence.

Yet, I know, when the noise subsides
I will find Your peace.
Teach me wisdom through these small observations of life,
And imprint on my heart the serenity
You offer a companion.

"Be still and know that I am God," instructs my favorite verse. But in practice my "object lesson" reveals just how difficult it is to hush my inner chatter. Have you learned to tame your stream of consciousness? Or does it always tumble rather noisily, skittering this way and that, caught up in the cares of your life, eddying around obstacles and splashing haphazardly from one thought to another? There is another way. You can seek another level of communication, descending into your own unruffled depths, into the sounds of silence. There in the stillness God offers a wordless embrace.

Do you dare to be a dropout from busyness? In our life today everyone is so preoccupied with looking and keeping busy. Being still has no priority for many people in our society. In fact, the converse is highly valued: being where the action is! The perception seems to be that if you're still, nothing is happening. If you're not making waves, nothing is flowing. And it appears so BORING—what good could possibly result from attempting to be quiet, subdued, hushed or silent?

Seeking the stillness seems to have a low priority in most lives. Yet time and time again the gospels tell us that Jesus went off by himself to pray. In the midst of the excited hubbub that he himself was causing, with his powerful preaching and his miraculous healings, Jesus went apart to be still. And as Jesus taught us, when the disciples asked him to teach them to pray, he responded with words that instruct us to praise God, seek God's will, ask for what we need daily, forgive others, and avoid temptation. And do all of this apart, secretly, in "a closet," in the stillness of our inmost hearts.

Still waters are important for spiritual growth. Evolution teaches us that God brought us forth from the great waters, and each of us is born from the waters of the womb. To seek that deep primordial place is to be reborn daily. In the silence of the quiet depths of prayer and meditation, God can instill in us the gifts of the Spirit. And we can sift through and distill matters lodged deep in our heart, casting aside all that constrains us from birthing something profoundly new.

PAT

HAVE A HEART

One day a word so troublesome came to me that I was tempted to ignore it—"just forget about it," said something inside me. Yet it had stopped my meditation with the characteristic urgency of other words that had been "given." That word was *suffuse.*

A foray into the dictionary was most unsatisfactory. The primary definition was "to overspread as with a color, liquid, etc.," taken from the Latin *suffundere*, meaning "to pour." My response: "So what?" How could this word connect me with a spiritual insight?

In my (limited) association with the word *suffuse*, I had always related it to "blush," envisioning the creeping pink tinge that envelops a person's whole body in a moment of embarrassment—a systematic reaction triggered by powerful emotions and emanating from the vital center of one's body.

That was it! I was rebelling against the idea that suffusion was just "poured on" from the outside, an outer coating changing one's exterior appearance. I rejected this seemingly shallow meaning for "my" word; I desired to view it as a thorough inundation, permeating to the core—not just superficially dripped over from the periphery. If something was "suffused with meaning," then it arose from being intrinsically important, not a mere after-coat of color.

Since my knee-jerk reaction to the definition of *suffuse* was so out-of-proportion, I suspected that I had hit on one of my spiritually sensitive areas: the mistaken premise that you can "put on" spirituality like a set of clothes. Some unwelcome images arose, like Paul's "armor of God" in Ephesians 6:13. Not only do I disavow the warlike metaphor for our time, but I reject the upside-down notion that you can clothe yourself with God's Spirit from the outside. Surely the attributes of truth, righteousness, peace, faith and salvation (all mentioned in this passage by Paul) must originate from our deepest heart of hearts. What is merely overlaid from the outside is no match for the surge of power that comes from within.

Paul speaks immeasurably better in Romans 5:5, reminding us that "God's love has been poured into our hearts through the Holy Spirit which has been given to us." Even before the scientific age, people intuitively claimed that the heart was the only true repository of God's love. We have all grown up with such phrases: "have a heart" implores us to show mercy; "learn by heart" urges us to move beyond mere brain-cell activity; the "heart of the matter" conquers all extraneous arguments to penetrate to the core meaning. Metaphorically, we invoke heart images to incorporate our ideals and values, to complete ourselves as sentient and responsive beings.

The heart remained in the realm of poets until the 18th century, when William Harvey theorized and then proved that central to our blood's circulation was the heart, the indispensable pump of a complicated distribution system. Day by day, minute by minute, our hearts beat, coursing blood throughout our bodies, tirelessly, all life long. The poured-in Spirit referenced by Paul pools in the heart and then is pumped out to all parts of our body, distributing love along with life itself.

This heart image is a powerful one for me. Often I pray with the psalmists for a clean heart (Ps. 51:10) or a heart of wisdom (Ps. 90:12). Sometimes, hoping to emulate Mary, I ask for a heart that magnifies the Lord—or, conversely, *is magnified by the Lord*—that I might contain all the love possible for the many hurting people in my pathway. And I desire, always, to hold those people I love close to my heart, to embrace them with a spiritual hug in prayer each day.

When I rewrote Psalm 51: 10-14 for my own use (a spiritual technique I recommend), I used these words:

Give me a thoroughly new heart
filled with light and love, O God;
Center me securely in your deep presence
and fill me to the brim with your Holy Spirit.
Teach me how to reflect your joy and saving grace;
Let your Spirit bubble up freely in me
and be a spa of love and mercy for others.

Only by such deep reflections of your Spirit
will my fellow-pilgrims be convinced
of your power and your goodness.
And they will be attracted to You . . . through me.
Make my new heart strong and unstained by sin
that my words on Your behalf will be mighty.

So . . . much did I learn from the word I almost rejected. Just as our failures rather than our triumphs are ultimately most instructive for us, sometimes a strong adverse reaction unleashes a new possibility that teaches us more than a comforting thought. The very word we struggle to "unwrap" for ourselves may be the one that has the most to disclose.

FALLOW, BE AT REST
PAT

AN ANTIDOTE TO MOTION

Of course it was inevitable that some of my given words would remain enigmas to me, despite meditation, dictionary searches and etymologies. Such a word was *fallow*.

Fallow. To me, fallow simply meant letting a field lie unplanted, unused for a time, in order to replenish itself in vital elements. Not too far from the authoritative, official definition—but a check in the dictionary did note one interesting refinement: the field was *plowed* before being left unplanted, specifically for a season or more. But there my rumination stopped. Dead-end.

The very next morning I received the word *rest*. Was God giving me a second chance? *Rest* seems so intimately connected with the word *fallow*. Letting soil lie fallow was a conscious decision to let the land rest for a time, to recuperate, to "do nothing" in preparation for a return to fullness and fruitful productivity.

Resting the land was a time-honored ancient custom observed in the Old Testament. In Leviticus the Hebrews were counseled to allow fields to lie fallow each seventh year. This law seemed to honor the land as the Hebrews honored the

Lord by resting on the seventh day—a kind of ecological sabbatical. And after seven times seven years, the Hebrews set aside the 50th year as a Jubilee year, a holy time signaled by the blowing of the ram's horn and commencing on the Day of Atonement. During the Jubilee year all field labor ceased, and the Hebrews also freed slaves and restored alienated lands to rightful owners. Ezekiel called it a "year of liberty" (Ezek. 46:17) and Isaiah named it a "year of redemption" (Isa. 63:4).

I wonder if we consider the fallow periods of our lives as times of liberty and redemption? More than likely, others, like myself, tend to place little value on the fallow times. Rather than resting in peace during such lapses in productivity, I am apt to become highly dissatisfied with my lack of fruitfulness. Instead of waiting, watching and resting peacefully I tend to seethe with impatience and discontent. Why? All because I do not trust the process. *Fallow* and *rest* equate to sloth in a mind that measures day by day—I forget to be mindful of the Mind that has created life to grow from seed to blossom to fruit—all in due time, in due season.

In our quest for boomerang gratification and measurable results, we disparage the attributes that only rest offers: healing and replenishment for our minds and bodies. In resting we let go of instant achievement and succumb to a slower, less perceptible process of physical and mental repair. Newborns excel at sleep and yet record phenomenal growth, but in adulthood we seek a different beat, an on-the-go persona that devalues rest and equates it with inertness.

As a young woman I discovered that being pregnant transformed my concept of rest. In the months of pregnancy rest became a totally positive non-activity: I needed and granted myself an inordinate amount of downtime. And being inactive did not stress me out—I was actually grateful for the excuse to accommodate my bulging Buddha-body with much more rest than usual. Deep within grew the consciousness that I could "do nothing" and yet be busily incubating precious life within. Gestation taught me to rest with gratitude—God was doing a new thing.

But I remember this singular consciousness precisely because it is so rare, so far removed from my usual reactions. With childbearing years a distant memory, now I must remind myself of the rest-full lessons learned during pregnancy: it's O.K. to have a portion of my life lie fallow as I tend to other fields. I remember that what now lies fallow has been plowed, turned up and ready to receive seeds, rain and sunshine. What appears to be idle is still working—working on renewing its strength and energies, preparing for future blooms. In fields or in ourselves, rest is not to be denigrated as useless, but celebrated as an essential rhythm of life. A Jubilee, in fact! It is all part of God's embedded wisdom in creation and its creatures.

Have we lost the biblical concept of *rest*? Our contemporary scene seems to have replaced rest with the pursuit of leisure (accent on *pursuit*!). When I look closely at many leisure-time activities, assiduously cultivated in work-free hours, I am tempted to say "give it a rest!" What passes for leisure is an almost frantic quest for entertainment and activities to occupy non-work hours. In stark contrast to the feeling of calm and tranquility in true rest, we instead sense that current-day leisure puts forth the image of being busily in motion, pervaded by a certain impatient uneasiness. *Rest*ive rather than *rest*orative is the adjective that comes to mind.

On to the etymological dictionary, where a quick look-up revealed that the word *rest* is derived from the Teutonic/

German root *rast*, with its original meaning related to "stage of a journey" or the Gothic *rasta*, which means "stretch of road." Revelation! Never had I connected *rest* with the word journey, but here it was, intimately intertwined at the roots with the phrase that many use to describe their life with God—a spiritual journey.

My understanding of the words *fallow* and *rest* assumes that productivity and activity have come before—that this quiet stage has followed a time of creativity, growth, ripening and harvesting. We recognize this cycle as well-embedded in nature, but we fail to apply it to the seasons of our personal lives, to give rest the place of honor it deserves. And this is our judgment despite all the scientific studies that offer indisputable proof of the critical and regular need for rest, each and every day.

In Matthew 11:28, Jesus says: "Come to me, all who labor and are heavy-laden, and I will give you rest." The kind of rest that Jesus offers is relief and freedom from anything that wearies, disturbs or troubles us. Jesus continues in 11:29: "Take my yoke upon you, and learn from me; for I am gentle and lowly in heart, and you will find rest for your souls."

Who among us does not need "rest for our souls," that blessed gift of mental and spiritual calm? Constant motion will not supplant that deep inner need for resting in God; as the wise counsel of St. Augustine instructs us, "You move us to delight in praising you; for you have formed us for yourself, and our hearts are restless till they find rest in you."

An old Southern folk tune says it so well:

For I am thine, I rest in Thee.
Great Spirit, come and rest in me.

So STOP. Just STOP. Stop the pursuit of leisure and reclaim rest. Rest by the side of the road along your journey. Be refreshed and renewed. Let parts of you lie fallow, and believe that God is still working as you rest. If you prepare the ground, God will come and plant seeds.

I rest my case!

PAT

GOD'S SENSE OF HUMOR

Today the word given in meditation was *laughter*. My reaction: "Are you kidding, Lord?" What could God be saying to me through this word? Could God be asking me to "lighten up," to take myself a bit less seriously, to be freer in expressing delight and pleasure?

How unusual to have this word surface—it doesn't seem very "spiritual." Yet clearly it was given to me this morning, possibly with a twinkle in God's eye. So I am bound to consider *laughter* seriously.

First, a confession. Seriousness comes naturally to me while laughter is not one of my salient characteristics. Perhaps, like many adults, I lost this gift as I aged, since it is apparent that laughter bubbles up effortlessly in the lives of children. Witness the merriment of youngsters making their own noisy, exuberant fun on a playground—and try *not* to smile! Their giggles and shouts fill the air with unmitigated glee and recreate in us the pure joy of living in the moment.

How sad that many of us "unlearn" laughter as we mature, except those rare and special people like my husband Bob, who have an irrepressible gift of humor that never fails to bring a smile, a chuckle, a laugh. It is he who points out the best of the comics page so that I begin breakfast with a smile;

and as he continues his detailed perusal of the daily newspaper (an indispensable aid to his starting the day off right!), he is a font of trenchant observations concerning the oddities of life and the human foibles he finds there. Laughter is our cheerful companion as we sip coffee and begin the day together.

The comics aren't the only bits of humor we share. Often I discover unexpected gifts tucked among the papers in my office: cartoons torn off from Bob's one-day-at-a-time calendar, featuring either Dilbert or the Far Side, two of his favorites. A good laugh is too precious to throw away without sharing!

When our children were young, to their chagrin I banned "The Three Stooges" from our home TV. The slapstick and often violent "humor" of Larry, Moe and Curly I found disturbing, though it was probably mild compared to the shows now viewed by children. The years have not changed my mind: if anything, my resistance to thoughtless inanity has stiffened as I age. And my negative opinion of this brand of humor also encompasses laugh-track situation comedies, stand-up comedians who try too hard to be funny, and other wags who offer elaborately-constructed jokes—all too contrived for my taste. Give me instead the spontaneous, unexpected banter that grows naturally from a real situation; in other words, something Bob would say!

From the list above, which I think of as "humorless humor," I exempt clowns. Clowns invite us to participate in jovial silliness, to forget our troubles and lose ourselves in simple delights. No wonder clowns are perennial favorites at the circus—we need their antics to bring forth guffaws to balance our cries of awe and fear as we watch performers on the high wire! In his book *Anatomy of an Illness*, the writer Norman Cousins tells us how he used the clowns in old movies to make him laugh as he was fighting a mysterious disease. As he discovered, laughter has beneficial physiological effects; in his case, laughter contributed to his healing and proved the old adage that "laughter is good medicine."

In a related world of make-believe, the theater, two masks have long been used as symbols representing the range of emotions portrayed: tragedy crying with a sad, turned-down mouth, and comedy laughing with a wide grin. Yet that is not the whole story: laughter itself has two faces. On one hand is laughter's innocent, happy face: a smile that is contagious and encourages good "vibes"; its obvious good humor brightens the laugher's whole disposition and the hearts of others who share the moment.

The second face of laughter does not emanate from happiness. Instead it has its source in murkier pools of emotion, in eddies of derision and scorn. Never in life is it fun to be laughed *at*, to be a laughing-stock, the butt of someone else's joke. Such laughter wounds, deeply and cruelly. No one is richer for it; we are all diminished, both the one ridiculing and the ridiculed. As Nietzsche opined in *Thus Spake Zarathustra*, "Not by wrath does one kill but by laughter."

To be able to laugh at one's self, however, may be a very positive outlet. Just think of people you know who lack this ability; they are deprived of a healthy sense of objectivity about themselves. Having the grace to laugh at our own self-righteous persona frees us from being crippled by our own ego; humor deflates vanity and allows our best self to shine through. Rightly used, self-laughter is an antidote to pride, a true gift from God.

I'm not talking here about nervous laughter, which springs from an entirely different source and betrays a lack of confidence. No. The self-laughter that brings us closer to God is the realization that at best we are still flawed creatures, never fully in control, dependent on God's providential care. That is the laughter of insightful self-growth.

Can you picture Jesus laughing? Perhaps at the wedding in Cana as he celebrated with friends and family? Maybe as he walked along with his disciples on the dusty roads of Judea and Galilee, or when he suddenly looked up and summoned Zacchaeus down from the sycamore tree? Surely, he laughed as he welcomed the children into his arms. A man with a mission must have a way to balance his serious task with the enjoyment of simple things: food, friends, even some frivolity. Laughter eases tension and leavens life with sweet bits of fun.

How do *you* get your daily dose of good laugh medicine? Are you lucky (as I am) to live with someone who nurtures you with humor? Do you read the comics along with your literary tomes? What do you do for fun? Conducting a laughter inventory in your life can be as revealing as taking a spiritual inventory. Jesus wept, says John 11:35, and, like Jesus, we all do our share of weeping in this life. But I also believe that Jesus laughed. And I believe that God enjoys our laughter, for life abundant and joyous is part of God's plan for each one of us.

PAT

HOLY GROUND

Laughter would be a hard word to follow. Seemingly so "unspiritual," it had reaped many thoughts about my relationship with God, others and myself. What would be God's next word-gift?

It came like a special offering: the word *sacred.* And my first thoughts had to do with the Lord's Supper, the phrase "set apart from a common to a sacred use." Common elements of bread and wine become a special sacrament, memorializing the sacrifice of Jesus Christ and empowering us who believe to share his spirit. Through ritual we leap from the common to the sacred in a matter of minutes, invoked by the words spoken and the hearts that respond.

The origin of the word *sacred* can be traced back through Middle English as *sacre,* "to bless," and is closely related to French's *sacrer* and Latin's *sacrare,* meaning "holy." In the same word family are sacrament, sacrifice, sacrilege, sacristan, sacrosanct. In each the "sacr" signals a holy beginning, though by the end of the word this holiness can be subverted, as it is, for example, in the word sacrilege (literally, "gatherer or stealer of sacred things"). Or, it can be enhanced, like the word sacrifice, which combines "sacri" (holy) with "facere" (make) to achieve "to make holy." In the word sacrosanct, we have a "double holy" meaning, reminiscent of the phrase "holy of holies," a place of special reverence.

In a retreat entitled "How Can I Keep from Singing?" the leader invited us to choose our favorite hymn and question ourselves about its significance: why did it have a paramount place of honor in our personal hymn lexicon? For me, the choice was a "no-brainer." Ever since grade school I harbored a special affinity for the hymn "Holy, Holy, Holy." But the question was *why*?

Combing through distant memories, I realized that "Holy, Holy, Holy" was probably the first Reformation hymn encountered in my Catholic girlhood. In the Catholic Mass I attended, only the choir sang, and certainly not (at that time) Protestant hymns! In our school assemblies we sang "Holy, Holy, Holy" frequently, and it forged a connecting link between my Saturday catechism class and my weekday academic pursuits. Joining in song with my classmates, I exulted in the repetitive "holy" word that enabled us all to praise One God together. Distinctions in religious traditions were subsumed as we shared this common music in our public auditorium. For that brief moment, secular and holy merged for me.

More recently "Sanctus" emerged as a meditation mantra, a repetitive and soothing means of clearing the mind of angst and busyness. Sung or intoned, "Sanctus" evokes stillness within and creates space for the holy. As John O'Donohue writes in *Anam Cara*: "To be holy is to be home, to be able to rest in the house of belonging that we call the soul."

Being holy is close to being whole. Both words, *holy* and *whole*, arise from the same Anglo-Saxon root, *hal*, which means "uninjured." Who do you know that has never been injured by life? No one, I would wager. Maybe the best we can do is to identify our wounds and pray for healing. That's why Henri

Nouwen calls us "wounded healers." We engage in serving and blessing others although we ourselves are not complete; we don't have all the answers or the right words, but we keep trying just the same . . . on our way to wholeness, and to holiness. Never arriving, but "walking the walk" anyway.

How do we decide what is "holy" in life, what is *sacred*? We can rely on tradition to point the way and designate rites, writings, places, events as holy: Holy Matrimony, Holy Bible, Holy Communion, Holy Orders. But can we go beyond tradition to stretch our idea of what is sacred?

Early in my life I thought I had a clear-cut idea of what was sacred, but my "clear-cut" idea was limited by what *others* designated as sacred. Sacred was the tabernacle where the hosts were stored on the altar, and sacred was the rite that consecrated the Eucharistic elements so that communicants could partake of them. My *sacred* telescope was focused on the church as a repository of the holy. And so it is—but not so exclusively as I once believed.

Now I focus on *sacred* with a wide-angle lens, and *sacred* takes in much more of the landscape. I see *sacred* more expansively, not only in the common elements shared at the Lord's Supper, but anywhere bread and wine are shared in love. Sacred moments abound, and holy ground is everywhere that God's Spirit pervades. The sacred seems embedded in the everyday, woven by God into the fabric of life itself. Who can single out the thread that is holy from all the others woven into your tapestry of life? Surely it is closely joined to all other threads that surround it, that cross it, that combine to make a beautiful design. Sacred is integral to the pattern, impossible to separate out. Life itself is sacred.

Can we as people be set aside from a common to a holy use? Can we present our bodies as the living sacrifice that Paul urges (Rom. 12:1), actually offering to make ourselves holy in God's eyes? Can we be so filled with love that we are consecrated to serve our fellow sojourners on this planet, or even beyond to the universe? Ages ago Hosea penned God's point of view: "For I desire steadfast love and not sacrifice, the knowledge of God, rather than burnt offerings." In slightly different words Micah (6:8) reiterated the same thing:

> *He has showed you, O man, what is good;*
> *and what does the Lord require of you*
> *but to do justice, and to love kindness,*
> *and to walk humbly with your God?*

Steadfast love, seeking the knowledge of God, and walking humbly in that knowledge, doing justice and being kind—pursuits declared sacred by God. Qualities found embedded in those who are holy, who bless others by their very being in all the ordinary days of life. Sacred gifts.

PAT

WHEN THINGS FLY APART

But I was not destined to remain in those places of light, dwelling with a "nice" and positive word such as *sacred.* Oh, no! The next word given was the antithesis of holy and wholeness, a word sent to shock me out of my blissful consideration of the sacred. The word was almost archaic: *asunder.*

In everyday speech the word *asunder* is rarely heard, so why did it suddenly appear as a word-gift? It definitely has an Old Testament ring to it, but I found only one reference, in Psalm 107:14, where the Israelites were recounting God's miracles of deliverance:

> *He brought them out of their darkness and gloom,*
> *and broke their bonds asunder.*

Divisive, fragmented, split into pieces, severely severed—those are my associations with *asunder*. It connotes a force that causes things to fly apart. How had this word all but disappeared from our modern lexicon? Had it been replaced by psychological jargon such as "fragmentation," which seems quite mild in comparison? *Asunder* is so much more definitive, has real heft to it, delivers so much more power. Why should so rare and strong a word dominate my meditation?

My journal reveals that this word appeared on a day when I felt splintered into many parts and stretched to my emotional limits. Over many months my husband Bob had been dealing with an acute and terribly painful attack of trigeminal neuralgia, a condition that is almost "off the charts" in terms of pain. (Look it up in the dictionary and you'll find the first word is "excruciating.") Though he bravely coped, he couldn't mask all the pain; it was almost impossible for him to speak, eat or swallow saliva without a searing jolt of nerve pain that hit like a neurological shock wave. That day, as he struggled to eat just a little, small sounds of his battle arose from the kitchen below, up to my meditation chair in the room above. Each muffled cry sent a small dagger through my heart.

In the clutches of such agony of witness to a loved one's suffering, my emotions rent me *asunder*. The integrated self that I had worked on for years to bring to a place of wholeness was split into many selves: the coping self, the angry self, the anxious self, the compassionate self, the sorrowful self, the despairing self—all seeking to dominate, not cooperate! "Divide and conquer" came to mind, as I lost my ability to withstand the emotional assault experienced.

In popular terminology, instead of "holding it all together," I "went to pieces." Tears alternated with rage, as first one self and then another gained the upper hand. In this extreme state of vulnerability, afloat in the chaos of my emotions, my shattered self could only turn to God in prayer. I needed God's love to reconnect those disparate selves, to bring together those fragments into something whole, to discern which to discard and which to nourish.

Asunder is a desperate condition. It feels like the aftermath of an earthquake, with everything a bit displaced from the upheaval. In the face of a crisis, certainties retreat, and our shadow side is sure to emerge to take full advantage of the psychic turmoil. Whoever said "crisis equals opportunity" used hindsight, because when you're in the midst of a crisis it's rare that such a rational thought occurs.

But the good news is that crisis *does* equal opportunity. In your upside-down state you can decide to tip towards regression or tip towards growth. By bringing our brokenness to God in prayer we begin the healing process, whether it be for grief, sorrow, loss, frustration, conflict within ourselves or with others.

Since Bob's trigeminal neuralgia is a chronic condition (for him it has lasted some 20 years), in my love for him I have known times of "asunder" more than I care to recall. During one time of his affliction, when an acute attack had dominated and disrupted our life for months, a spiritual friend named Susan discerned the despair in my voice and asked, "Do you think it would help to write a psalm?" Instantaneously my heart said "yes." Why hadn't I birthed this idea myself? In writing I always find solace, and I knew that a psalm of lament would express my agitated feelings better than any other literary form. Here is the psalm I wrote:

Dread is my companion as I awake from a restless night's sleep;
Fear compresses my soul.
Can I face another day of watching Bob's pain?
My innards shake at the prospect.

Arise I must, despite dread and fear;
To face a loved one's anguish is my calling.
If Bob is peacefully sleeping in his chair, I give thanks;
If he already is struggling with jolts of pain, my heart shrinks within me.

I go through the motions of domesticity:
I make the coffee, fetch the newspapers.
This is the outer extent of my caregiving,
For to touch my beloved only brings more pain.

So I circle around the problem,
Seeking to be a caring presence,
Trying not to weep, at least not in front of Bob.
Pretending to handle our situation, even as my heart breaks.

How long, O Lord? I cry with the psalmist.
Is there no end to pain, no solution that works for good?
We have been in this pit now for 10 weeks;
Where is the light at the end of the tunnel?

If joy comes with the morning, where is the sunrise for us?
We search for answers, but there are only more questions.
So much history, and still a mystery.

You have been our strong presence in the past;
We pray now that Your love will overcome the pain,
The fear, the dread that fills our lives.

Hear our prayers, O God;
Feel our pain and dismay.
Let Your light pierce this darkness
And bring us comfort and hope.

Through prayer God gives us the strength to "pick up the pieces"—all those fragments of our hurting self—and put ourselves back together, with God's love as the glue. No one wishes for the suffering that comes from being *asunder*, but the process of recovery enables us to reassemble the pieces, perhaps into new patterns closer to God's image of our innermost soul.

Maybe this is why Jesus leads off his beatitudes with "Blessed are the poor in spirit, for theirs is the kingdom of heaven." When you are asunder, you are "poor in spirit." You know to your depths how needy you are for God's presence; no longer do you feel self-sufficient, in control, full of rugged individualism. *Asunder* often stands at the center of life's great turning points. And it is just at that very point, when all defenses are down, that God can enter in most powerfully.

If we were never asunder, could we possibly appreciate times of wholeness and harmony? The crises of life cause us to clothe ourselves with new perceptions; our vision is permanently widened and sharpened, never again to narrow and blur all our experiences as "ordinary." Suddenly, all is gift. Sometimes only by experiencing opposites can we come to appreciate all the everyday blessings that go unrecognized day by day.

No, I do not go in search of sundering—who would? But when it comes, as it sometimes must to any life, I trust that God will be there with me, willing me to a new level of wholeness and guiding me on the pathway.

PAT

A QUESTION OF SURVIVAL

For the first time since beginning this book, I chose to skip over a word that had been revealed. Instead I tackled the next word and intended to ignore the previous troublesome word. But once I finished that other word, my conscience pulled me back with a nagging question: If in my writing I was "unwrapping" these words as I would a gift, why would I opt to leave one forever sealed? So I confronted the word *survive*.

Survival seems a most rigorous test when external pressures ally themselves with internal struggles, like two arms of a pincer movement, to create a massive "squeeze-play" in the psyche. The day that *survive* presented itself in my meditation, I know I was feeling beset by just such a villainous embrace. Externally, I was plagued by being forced to witness a return bout of my husband's painful chronic illness, which turns our happy home into a house of pain. Simultaneously, on the inner front I was grasping for a handhold to help me surmount the turmoil of scaling a new spiritual mountain. I was figuratively "holding on for dear life" while a number of time-honored "sure things" died and I awaited the birth of something new. To endure the pain encircling me inside and out, I had brought forth the word *survive*... and then opted to avoid it.

Why avoid *survive*? After all, it is basically a positive, non-threatening word. It means to remain alive after the death of someone, the cessation of something, or the occurrence of some event. Something to celebrate, right? In life we often are happy to survive . . . a loss, a downturn, a fall, a decline, or even a destructive relationship. And yet *survive* has a strong shadow side. By implication, it hints of dire difficulty and the real possibility that others *didn't* survive but instead succumbed to adverse circumstances.

For instance, in the wake of the WWII holocaust, psychologists noted a prevalent affliction called survivors' guilt, a deep-seated pain that tortured those who had escaped death in the concentration camps. "Why me?" they asked—not as the psalms of lament ask about the negative events leading to suffering—but "why me?" in relation to this positive happening, their survival. In a way they were crying "why *not* me?" Why did *I* survive when so many perished? What can it mean for me to have survived against such incredible odds?

No one could answer this anguished cry of the victims of the holocaust. The "why" questions of faith are rarely answered, since they are locked in the mystery of God's realm. The best you can do is to grapple with these issues for yourself and come to some conclusions about what survival means to your future life, the actions you will take, and the way you will choose to treat others.

To survive you need many qualities: faith, endurance, persistence, willpower, courage, creativity, a "nevertheless" attitude, energy and guts—to mention a few. And more than a little luck. These characteristics must have been deeply at work in the lives of the holocaust survivors, just as they are in the lives of many people we meet in the course of our daily rounds, people trying to survive the ordeals by fire of ordinary life: a broken marriage, a devastating illness, a catastrophic accident, bedeviling memories, dysfunctional relationships. In whatever way they can, they are trying to live through difficulties that have dramatically turned their lives upside-down.

This "living through" aspect of crises leads me to suggest a new word, "transvive," as a substitute for survive. *Sur*vive literally means to "over live" (from the French verb *survivre* or Latin's *supervivere*); *trans*vive acknowledges the reality of having to *walk though* our problems to get to the other side. Whereas with *sur*vive the connotation seems to be that one leaps over the problems and suffering in life to arrive untouched and unscathed beyond them, *trans*vive admits to all the steadfast and courageous plodding that must go on in the midst of the trials to land safely in a new place. It's in harmony with Robert Frost's comment (discovered one day on a greeting card): "The best way out is always through."

For when people walk through a time of suffering, they are never the same person they were before; they have been forever changed, perhaps radically so, transformed by their experience. Perhaps they awaken to a new depth of spirituality. Or the shake-up alerts them to new capacities and insights about themselves. Having experienced life at the edge, they may embrace a deeper connectedness with others—or may feel a more profound sense of isolation. The individual variations are endless but one constant remains: passing through the storm has reconstituted them as a new entity.

Of course, when the stormy waters rage, we each need our life preservers, those people who will journey with us through the waves and support us as we swim to the other side. They enable us to keep our heads above the waters, encourage us not to grow weary or capitulate, bring us hope as a companion, and offer steadiness and reliability as a counter to despair. As we struggle not to give in to the deep waters and go under, they keep us afloat by their caring. They adopt the position stated by Leonard Sweet in his book *A Cup of Coffee at the Soul Café*: "Our duty is not to see through one another but to see one another through."

In a very real sense we are all survivors . . . and we are all life preservers. The experience of one feeds the experience of the other. Life calls on us to be ready to survive ourselves and to help others survive. There's a "we-ness" to survival: in the song line of an old hymn, the "we shall overcome" phrase epitomizes the triumph of the human spirit and the bonds of unity that are forged by facing a common enemy or linking up to bolster a common cause. With a little help from those who reach out with God's love, we can transvive anything.

PAT

A PASSAGEWAY

If there's one thing in the world I do *not* want to be, it is *narrow*, as in narrow-minded. Narrow people are those that adopt a one-track mentality, walking within carefully-prescribed areas limited to "their own kind"; people of constricted spirit, they eschew contact with others who are different and prefer the exclusive company of those who share their opinions. As a descriptive word, *narrow* elicits only negative vibrations when applied to a person's mind or views—only rarely does it describe a desirable quality, as in narrow-waisted (in my case, long lost and wistfully remembered!).

Yet one morning *narrow* was my word, my field to plow, my ore to mine. In response, I queried: "Why this word, *narrow*, when I think I'm supposed to be expanding in knowledge and spirit?" Mining any positive nuggets from such a negative word would require lots of digging.

In Luke 13:24, Jesus says: "Strive to enter by the narrow door, for many, I tell you, will seek to enter and not be able." Matt. 7:13 echoes and enlarges this thought:

> *Enter by the narrow gate; for the gate is wide and the way is easy, that leads to destruction, and those who enter it are many. For the gate is narrow and the way is hard, that leads to life, and those that find it are few.*

True enough for Jesus, but for me? Both these passages are a bit scary and offputting for anyone standing on the threshold of a door, or reaching for that latch on a gate! The symbolism brings to mind *The Road Less Traveled* alluded to by M. Scott Peck in his book by the same name, a rather formidable way closed to all but stouthearted, dedicated souls who dare to be different.

It takes some careful maneuvering to get in and out of narrow places. One I particularly remember was a rocky passage named "the lemon-squeezer" in a cave in New Hampshire. We were visiting the area with our three children, exploring the labyrinthine pathways, when we came upon the challenge of the lemon-squeezer. Of course the children were small enough to slide through the miniscule aperture with delight, and they gleefully watched as the adults had to opt for the longer, more tortuous route that bypassed the narrow spot. Similarly, in life, children can often avoid traversing the more complicated sophistry of adulthood and exult in taking the most direct and straightforward route.

As a generalist by nature, I've always chosen to embrace a wide range of activities rather than to constrict my focus to a narrow specialty; in fact, for years I put off writing for fear that it would consume me in the narrow way, squeezing out all those other important priorities and people I value. But perhaps, in today's world of exponentially-exploding choices, to narrow down this wide array of opportunities to a reasonable number of options may be the only recourse to avoid being overwhelmed by distractions. Paring down the plethora of possibilities may be the way of wisdom that Jesus meant. *Narrow* as a verb, as in "to narrow down" is light-years away from *narrow* as an adjective!

But some things we try to narrow down are the very things that we are called to expand in our spiritual life. We prefer to cram God into little boxes of rituals and rules—God is so much more manageable in a narrow place! It has something to do with our need to possess God, rather than expand ourselves to join in God's Spirit. We mistakenly try to cut down God to earthly "life-size" instead of celebrating the creative immensity of God's universal power. We selfishly intone "God is in my heart" rather than "I am in the heart of God."

Years ago I read J.B. Phillips's book, *Your God Is Too Small*, in which he tries to scuttle the various images of God that are truly too narrow to live by. He names various prototypical God-images carried over from childhood—"resident policeman," "God-in-a-box," "grand old man" are among my favorite titles—dissects them, and urges us to work to expand these lesser versions of God in order to arrive at a God who is unlimited, One who is completely adequate and real for the challenges of adulthood.

Then my meanderings with *narrow* took me down an entirely different fork in the road. Way down in the definitions for the adjective *narrow* stands another meaning with a more positive thrust: "careful or minute." What if following Jesus' admonishment "strive to enter by the narrow door" was calling us to a new vision, one clearly focused to lift us to a heightened mindfulness that would cause us to pay attention to details rather than taking them for-granted? Or to reach for an in-the-moment awareness that would have us meditating on the daily ordinary gifts of God, extracting meaning from the minute and enlarging it philosophically? In careful ponderings of small happenings, could such "narrowness" enlarge our consciousness?

Most of us do not tread the boards of a worldwide stage. Rather, we inhabit a narrower sphere of influence, one in which we must take to heart Mother Teresa's advice: we cannot do great things, but only small things with great love. What wise and epigrammatic philosopher said "God is in the details"?

In this "narrow door" metaphor Jesus calls us to scrutinize our everyday actions, search our deepest hearts, and inquire carefully about our motivations—an examination that has much in common with Jesus' experience of being tempted in the wilderness as he considered his own ministry on earth. He chose the narrow door of compassion, the narrow gate of forgiveness; entering them he walked the way of sacrifice and arrived in God's own realm of eternal life. And we are invited to follow him.

Each Sunday I am pleased to read and ponder this prayer, placed weekly at the top of the worship bulletin: "O God, make the door of this house wide enough to receive all who need human love and fellowship, narrow enough to shut out all envy, pride, and strife." Now, that's a *narrow* I can espouse and celebrate! May it be so at the doorways of all our churches and other institutions, and at the gates of our businesses and schools in our wider society. And may we each strive to banish envy, pride and strife from crossing the doorways of our own homes. Then we will be truly blessed.

PAT
FAREWELL

SAYING OUR GOOD-BYES

For many years there was no cessation from the business-as-usual routine of our family-owned enterprise, a consulting/software company. Work-weeks were predictable—long, stressful, demanding. A departure from the norm would have been most welcome, but the grind was relentless and the pressure unremitting.

In contrast, retirement has frequently brought us to the point of departure, as we regularly leave for long-postponed tours of distant lands. So much have we traveled during the last few years, in fact, that leave-taking has become a frequent event for us, so when *departure* surfaced as a word in meditation one morning, my musings jump-started many associations.

Departure necessitates letting go of the known and the familiar, changing the pattern, deviating from the norm, diverging from the usual—all of which I do poorly. Therefore departure is traumatic for me: here I am at the point of embarking on a journey, and not only do all the preparations for the future need careful thought, but I insist that all I'm leaving behind must also be in good order. Talk about a squeeze play!

And I am not just speaking about practical matters, such as arrangements for the mail and newspapers and other household cares, but other preparations as well: all those personal contacts, friends and family, who must be apprised of our whereabouts by itineraries; and even ultimate business matters, like wills and financial records, which must be in a state of perfect completion. You can understand, with this mindset, why I am not good at good-byes, and only fair at farewells!

It helps to know that I am not alone in my leave-taking compulsions. A good friend of mine confesses to the same frantic and unreasonable syndrome: she too must surmount incredible "to do" lists, and see each of her children face-to-face before taking off. We both suffer from this imprinted ritual that creates a strong sense of unease if certain self-imposed conditions are not met before we say our good-byes.

Perhaps a vacation departure deadline avails one more chance to tidy up our affairs, to seek closure amidst all the ongoingness of our lives. We are stepping out beyond the flow of our ordinary days, to take some risks, to travel over new terrain—and my preparations become as frantic as a squirrel scurrying around making sure it's ready for winter hibernation. Only the finality of D-Day (Departure Day) makes me cease and desist from my busyness.

Differences in departure rituals are particularly notable between married couples. This disparity was graphically demonstrated one evening by means of a simple exercise facilitated by our minister for a church group. She asked that we divide into two groups: one for those who are usually *first* to leave a party, and the other for those who are usually among the *last* to depart. In every case, the married couples in the group ended up being separated from each other: one in the "first to leave" segment and the other in the "last to depart" contingent. This scenario usually plays out with the lingerer acting as the immovable object and the other married partner taking the role of the irresistible force!

What deep personality characteristics cause such variations in our ways of departure? Do the "first to leave" have a stronger internal clock, a more decisive nature? Do the "last to depart" see the need for one more exchange, or one more word of thanks to the host? Analyzing one's habits surrounding departure can lead not only to copious laughter, but to many personal insights as well. Departure stimulates a full and complex gamut of emotions: from sorrow to anticipation, from anxiety to excitement, from conflict to peace.

When you reach the decade of your 70's, as I have, you cannot help speculating about the circumstances of your own final departure from this world. Either consciously or subconsciously, questions buzz, especially those tried-and-true basic questions embedded from my journalism training, the five W's and one H: *who, what, when, where, why* and *how.*

What event will take me from this earthly existence? *When* and *where* will it occur? *Who* will be with me? *How* will I handle the reality of my own demise? Only *why* is not a feasible question but a foregone conclusion—because we are mortal that's why, and death comes to everyone.

But not everyone comes to terms with death. In my family, for example, my father was constantly haunted by one question: "How will it all end?" Already in his 80's, he feared a long drawn-out illness of incapability and dependence. He prayed for a quick exit, and he mercifully got his wish: a diagnosis of colon cancer one week, a final breath the next. Just the abrupt departure he desired.

The experience of aging teaches us that mortality, once an abstract concept, becomes increasingly personal. The years tick by, and you begin to incorporate viscerally the sure knowledge that the time for your departure is imminent, and growing inexorably nearer each day. In one sense, your days grow more precious; in another sense, you realize you must be prepared to let go of this life, of this world, and you pray for grace to enable your passage.

Perhaps the incremental losses of the aged—the deaths of loved ones, the diminution of physical and mental powers, the limitations of a body growing ever frailer through various diseases and disorders—teach us some truth about the final relinquishment, death. You accede that your body has waned as you have stored up rich memories through the years. In many ways, long life is a trade-off: less physical prowess for experiential richness. Would you really wish to be a teenager again, with hormones raging, coping with the dichotomy of feeling angst about the future while declaring with bravado that the world is yours for the taking? Or is it more peaceful to meditate on what was, and give thanks for that youthful passage even as you embrace your current stage of life and become ready to depart?

In the story of Jesus' transfiguration on the mountain (Luke 9:30-31), the central subject of conversation recorded was Jesus' departure from earth:

> *And behold, two men talked with him, Moses and Elijah, who appeared in glory and spoke of his departure, which was to be accomplished at Jerusalem.*

Ignoring this message, Peter's response was to suggest installing three tents, so Jesus could put down stakes right where he was. Forget all that talk about departure! But later, as Peter himself awaits martyrdom, he recalls this moment of Transfiguration in 2Peter1: 15 and instructs his followers:

> *And I will make every effort to see that after my departure you will always be able to remember these things.*

Since the mountaintop experience, Peter has made the long journey from holding on to letting go; he has embraced the inevitability of his own departure.

My husband and I, married 50 blessed years, have followed Peter in coming to that turn of the road where we accept the reality that we are nearing our last chapter. Our life has been full of love shared during both sadness and joy. To have known such love on earth is to have tasted heaven. Departure from each other will be full of pain, but the promise of our faith assures us that we will be together in our final homecoming.

PAT

A TIME APART

I am on a personal, unstructured retreat, experiencing a "holy respite," a break from life-as-usual. As I traveled to this quiet place, just to *be*, I wondered which of my many words would surface to be "the" word for these days of writing. And the word was *time*.

Time has such a relational quality. In reality, it ticks on inexorably, second by second. Yet it has a keen dependency on you and your current circumstances for its perception. In a moment of terror or disaster, time can literally seem to stand still. Who has not experienced entering a time warp state-of-mind where you perceive everything happening as a slow-motion scene of a movie? Conversely, especially in times of joy, such as the wedding of your child after months of planning and preparation, you are apt to enter an experience of the event careening by in "double-time": the big day rushes by on fast-forward and you are left stunned by the fact that it's already over.

Even at normal times free of obvious stress or joy, time can be perceived entirely differently by individuals sharing a common experience. At a recent retreat, for instance, the leader offered a guided meditation as part of our prayer time, and I thought her pace was perfect: enough silent time between each section to afford fruitful thoughts, yet not so slow as to be soporific.

Afterward I was surprised to hear several people dissent from my view of her timing: some complained that she proceeded too fast for their processing; others, of course, claimed that the time dragged on and on, much too long. These latter voices, from those whose inner alarm clocks are set to respond at an instant's notice, could not acclimate themselves to a more measured use of time for pondering. We each bring an inner sense, probably developed early in our life, that dictates how we respond to the passage of time.

Children learn to develop a sense of time because adults work hard to teach the concept to them. In the beginning infants assault our idea of a regular timetable, often turning our nights into day, and vice versa. Even the most permissive parent gradually works toward regulating the infant to a schedule that's kinder to adult sleep patterns. As the child grows to be a toddler, he hears the repetitive phrase "time for bed" each evening and (hopefully!) begins to internalize the parent's sense of appropriate timing.

In our family history we have a favorite story about our eldest son's use of time for his own advantage. When he was almost two, my mother-in-law came to care for him while I was hospitalized for the birth of a second baby. For her comfort level about our son's usual schedule, I had written out some notes so she would know what to expect on a daily basis. Depending on this list pretty heavily and consulting it frequently, she would point to it and cheerily inform him in a no-nonsense voice, "Time for a nap." Quick to sense her reliance on this source for her authority, our son climbed up on a chair to reach the list that grandmother was constantly quoting, pointed dramatically to it and announced, "Time for a cookie!"

In the company of a special friend, time itself can take on a timeless quality. Fortunately, in my lifetime I have experienced this blessed state with several "soul friends." Yes, of course we discuss worldly issues, decisions and events, and we also talk of personal joys and concerns. But somewhere between the words spoken, we reach a place where timelessness reigns. One such friend captured this serendipity in a banner she designed and fabricated for me:

When two souls meet within God's heart,
Time stands still . . .
And eternity has been proven.

In another century, the German mystic Jakob Boehme offered these words: "He to whom time is the same as eternity, and eternity the same as time, is free of all adversity."

But for most of us, most of the time, time *is* adversity. It's no secret that most adults in the workaday world feel extremely pressured by time—time is "the enemy." In my position as editor in a fast-moving, high-tech industry, I measured time from one deadline to the next; the pressure of time seemed essential to make things happen as we strove to turn out a finished product to deliver to a client. The clock became not just a recorder of the minutes and hours, but a stern dictator demanding that you report in for duty every hour on the hour (or maybe in more frequent increments than that!).

So it was inevitable that my time on retreat should assume an entirely different quality. Instead of marching, time began to waltz slowly. It stretched out languorously and developed some blurred edges, like the view from my retreat-house window: a vista of the sea meeting the horizon of the sky, with an indistinct point of touch in the distance. Intellectually I knew I was dealing with the same old ticking clock, but perceptually and viscerally I felt I was inhabiting a different space. My spirit slowed and expanded as I realized anew with Ecclesiastes that I indeed had "a time for every matter under heaven" (Ecc. 8:6).

In a serendipitous example of synchronicity, one of my morning readings happened to offer these words of encouragement:

> *Giving yourself plenty of time is a simple but vital exercise: Leave all agendas behind you. Let the neglected presence of your soul come to meet and engage you again.*

This advice brought to mind an incident from several years ago, when I was resident at a three-week course in spiritual direction in New York City. On our schedule was a weekend retreat in the nearby countryside, and I was busily stowing numerous books into my suitcase in anticipation of time to spend on an academic project. Just then my free-spirited neighbor from the next room popped in. In contrast to my bulging suitcase, hanging from her shoulder was a small knapsack—the sole piece of luggage she was bringing on retreat. "I am just going to waste time with God," she merrily reported. Immediately I was struck by her lightness of spirit and freedom, her great delight at the prospect of an open agenda with God. Only later did I realize how wise she was, how unencumbered. To waste time with God is a "simple but vital" exercise avoided by many of us goal-oriented types. The lesson: approach God full of expectation but don't take along a lot of extraneous baggage.

Wasting time gets short shrift in our culture. For every saying that urges us to slow down ("take time to smell the roses"), there are two that counter-attack: "time waits for no one" or "time's a-wastin'." We're more likely to hear "it's about time!" said impatiently than the compassionate "take your time." "Time is money" rules our life, as do timetables and time-sensitive materials. In such a society WWJD (what would Jesus do)?

Have you ever been struck by the seeming time*lessness* of Jesus? Although he felt himself on a mission, he had time for all in his pathway, stopping to preach and teach, to heal and pray, to tell stories and welcome the children, to touch others and give them hope. His words also have a timeless quality. Even though he spoke in simple stories to those in an agrarian society 2000 years ago, his metaphors have the power to touch us today.

The concordance yields only one reference to Jesus quoting time, Matt. 26:18:

> *He said, "Go into the city to a certain one, and say to him, 'The teacher says, my time is at hand; I will keep the Passover with my disciples.'"*

Earthly time was drawing to a close for Jesus, and he wanted to use his last moments well.

Jesus' gift was his ability to infuse chronological time with moments of "kairos," eternal time. So deep was his connection with God that his time here was unfettered by space and place. Small moments in his short life have become of great moment to us. His time in the realm of the Spirit was well spent. And so can ours be.

To quote an old lyric, say to the Lord, "my time is your time."

God's gift to us is time and space. And our return gift to God is the same—time in prayer and service, and space for his Word to be planted in us, for growth, bloom and reaping . . . all in due time.

PAT

TAKING THE PLUNGE

When the word is *deep*, there is nothing else to do but plunge in! And what better place than Genesis?

> *In the beginning God created the heavens and the earth.*
> *The earth was without form and void, and darkness was upon the face of the deep;*
> *and the Spirit of God was moving over the face of the waters.*
> (Gen. 1:2)

For eons the ocean's other name has been "the deep." The image that arises is a place of fathomless depth, of dark and mysterious unknown forms of life. Not a fit habitat for man, who needs light and air, yet somehow we are drawn to those depths and believe that our own distant origins developed there.

In these days of submersible labs and automated cameras that dive and penetrate the deep as never before, we are vastly improving our knowledge of the swarming underworld of diverse life resident in our oceans. But those who choose to be marine adventurers are an exclusive minority—the rest of us are more likely to keep our heads above water (with the rest of our bodies!) because it's absolutely scary to encounter the mysterious depths of such an alien kingdom.

Many of us find the same difficulty in exploring our own depths, and for the same reason: it's scary. In those depths swim mysterious thoughts, strange undercurrents, elusive feelings, supercharged memories, unresolved conflicts—and we'd just as soon *not* fish them out. Yet, do you remember what Jesus told Simon Peter (Luke 5:4)?

"Put out into the deep and let down your nets for a catch." Peter protests, but does it anyway. And behold! What a catch they netted. Not just the fish but a whole new way of life was the result, as Peter and his partners James and John became "fishers of men."

We are expert avoiders of this kind of obedience and conversion. Not only do we avoid our own deep places, but we skirt about those areas in others. We don't want to "get in too deep" with the problems of our neighbor, our friend, our colleague. We'll wade about the edges, perhaps, but strive to keep our heads above someone else's deep waters.

Even people in a caregiving ministry are more comfortable defaulting to continuous small talk that goes with "visiting" instead of leading the person into an in-depth exchange. Recently in our church's caregiving group we invited a hospice chaplain to enlighten us on how to open up the suffering person to engage in significant sharing. Entitled "Deeper Conversations," his presentation offered questions designed to touch various areas of life in order to break through the chitchat level into a more profound dialogue. His questioning techniques were really quite simple, ranging from "what are you thinking about?" to "what are you praying for?" and "where is God for you right now?" The real crux of his expertise was not the question asked but how he was able to handle the answers received; he heard contemporary laments that rivaled the feelings of some old psalms: *"Out of the depths, I cry to thee, O Lord"* (Ps. 130:1). It takes courage to touch such a tender spot and be a non-anxious presence to people in pain.

You can cultivate your ability to be such a non-anxious presence to others. Like everything else, it just takes practice.

In my daily quiet time I go to such a nurturing place in my imagination. It is my garden sanctuary, reminiscent of the original Garden of Eden, filled with flowers and trees and creatures . . . and peace. It is there that I meet Jesus, and we sit companionably by the side of a great lake, a very deep lake of serenity. In prayer I open my heart, assured that the spirit of Jesus will give a compassionate response. Nothing is prohibited or off-limits; all is acceptable. I can both empty out and fill up my depths. And I leave with enough love to last one day, filled with the living water Jesus offers, plenty for myself—and more than enough to overflow into the lives of others.

If you are to be effective in helping others, nurturing yourself in prayer and meditation is not an option, it is a necessity. Seeking a state of composure is best done in the "non-anxious" presence of God. In that good company we bring together the elements of our lives and ask God to form a good whole out of the many pieces of our life. In printing terminology, we are literally "setting the type" of our experience or, in musicology, putting the notes together to compose our song. We are taking time to sift through the many areas of our life to reveal patterns that enlighten our own behaviors to ourselves, and culling insights that may contribute to our understanding and support of others.

Deep down we know that thoughts fraught with meaning will emerge from our own depths if we but still ourselves to hear the voice of God. Take time to invite God to be a deep third eye with a powerful lens of inner perception for you. Enter into your depths trusting that the Holy Spirit will open some doors that have been barricaded shut; have faith that God will show you insights and startle you with delightful surprises.

"Deep in my heart, I do believe . . ." goes the old spiritual, so breathe deeply and take the plunge. It's refreshing.

SELF
SELF
WORK
HOME
WORK
SELF
HOME
SELF
WORK
HOME
FAMILY
DREAMS
FAMILY
DREAMS
PAT

HANGING IN THE BALANCE

Have you ever viewed your life and decided you were trying to perform an impossible balancing act? Striving to be centered but always listing to one side or another? Trying to decide with equity how to juggle all the facets of your life without all the pieces crashing down about you? Knowing that you must choose one side of the seesaw to put your weight on and wondering whom that will leave stranded up in the air?

I thought early on that I would stumble on a clear way to divide myself (now there's an image!) between marriage and career, wife and mother, goals and people. But instead I always seem to be facing the challenge of staying on the balance beam as the force of gravity beckons me to fall off one side or the other. Finding that perfect stillpoint, that place of inner equilibrium where all is properly aligned, is a state seldom reached and *never* sustained.

Balance was a shoo-in, a sure thing, to be one of my given words.

But then I received another gift in meditation—not just a word, a whole phrase: "Jesus, the fulcrum of my life." Of course I jolted to a jarring stop. "Fulcrum," I thought, "I even forget the definition, not to mention any other fuzzy memories from physics!" So off to the dictionary for a personal update: *fulcrum* is defined as "the support, or point of rest, on which a lever turns on moving a body"; or, more simply, "any prop or support."

Why, it was a perfect fit! Jesus the Christ is the main support of my spiritual journey, a dependable source of wisdom. I believe we have a synergistic interdependence: I surely need him as a teacher, guide and companion, and he depends on me (and lots of other folks!) to be his hands, eyes, ears and heart in this world. That's my interpretation of being "in Christ," to incarnate in myself all that he tried to teach us to do and to be.

And there's no doubt that he props me up many times a day as my balancing act proceeds. Even more marvelous, he can help each person to achieve that elusive stillpoint no matter her size, weight and responsibilities—because surely God loves the challenge of diversity! My idea of a balanced life may make no sense at all to many others; each has to discover for herself what centers her and keeps her on the beam. Without personal reflection, how can we discern the fine lines between self-confidence/arrogance, spiritual power/self-righteousness, what is selfish/unselfish, proper use of power/exploitation? Narrow is the beam we walk between such "opposites," because in reality we slip from one side to the other with great ease.

One of the pillars of the Christian faith who models a balanced way is St. Benedict (b. 480), in his master work "The Rule of St. Benedict." Centuries ago in his community he sought to achieve a balance of interdependence and personal responsibility among the monks of the Order. In addition, he encouraged a daily pattern of study, work and prayer; note the incorporation of mind-body-spirit—St. Benedict may be the first proponent of a holistic approach to life. And these elements were not rigidly separated in the community's following of the Rule, rather they were a smooth blending of the sacred and the mundane, equally valued for their contributions to the spiritual life.

In a typical day, the proportion recommended by the Rule was study—4 hours, prayer—4 hours, and work—6 hours; a fair share must have been reserved for sleep! And that's wise, too.

When I consider my days in the light of Benedict's teachings, I see immediately how easy it is to get out-of-whack. In no way does my daily schedule approach his even-handed proportions . . . but I can try to adjust the balance to tilt a bit more to the prayer and study elements, and I can endeavor to adapt my priorities so that my work allows for such a moderate adjustment.

The structure we give our lives reflects that which we value. What we add or what we let go speaks volumes about the kind of person we are and want to be. Do I really want concentrated time for writing? Then I can let the message machine handle the telephone for a morning. Am I positive that my ministry is to be responsive to people in trouble? Then I will answer the telephone immediately. The sticky wicket arises when we find ourselves at cross-purposes, choosing not between good and evil, but two "goods." Yes, I want to write, and yes, I want to be available to others.

That's when I turn to Jesus, my point of rest, in prayer. He's my fulcrum, ever ready to move me along and prop me up. He supplies the leverage that is necessary to negotiate the tightrope of conflicting priorities and competing goals without falling off the wire! I also use one of my favorite verses (Ps. 51:6) as a repetitive mantra:

Behold, Thou desirest truth in the inward being;
therefore teach me wisdom in my secret heart.

And then I wait for God to right the balance.

PAT

A MEASURE BEYOND TIME

I took a walk this morning. Not unusual, those who know me would say. But it was. A combination of traveling, ill health and cold weather had kept me from following this ordinary habit. This morning, however, the sun was beckoning, and—for January—the temperature was rather balmy. The breeze fluttered between gentle and forceful but was never bitterly cold—always a breeze, never a wind.

So I bundled up in layers and sallied forth. Given that I was out of practice for demanding exercise, I hoped I could at least walk part way to the pond, my preferred destination. Half a walk is better than none, I told myself, ready to settle for less than I desired.

To my surprise, some unexpected energy kicked in and propelled me all the way to the pond, my special place of reflection. Diligent in my pursuit of the sun, I declined to sit on my "meditation rock," which was shrouded by the morning shade; I opted to stand in the sunshine as I beheld the pond in all its wintry glory.

Gone were the remembered brilliant reflections of autumn, and in their place stood the black tracery of trees silhouetted against the pale blue sky. The waters of the pond were divided: only half the water still ran freely to capture the image of trees against sky, the other portion was covered with white, snowy ice. No animal life disturbed the near-perfect stillness of the scene.

I stood transfixed. It was a *moment.*

Have you ever felt yourself transported by standing before an object or a scene? Stunned by a beautiful piece of art, perhaps . . . or by the breathless panorama of a pink-and-purple sunset . . . or the hypnotic, ever-breaking waves at the seashore. Awe and wonder well up as a deep, heartfelt response; gratitude comes in on the tide.

Moment reared itself as one of my words long ago. What is a *moment*? A blip in time, but not a means of time. A *moment* has no chronological measure: its length is defined by each person's experience. My "moment" at the pond was completely subjective. I'm sure that inhabitants of passing cars wondered at my stock-stillness as I gazed so fixedly at an ordinary winter landscape.

Of all words, *moment* has the widest possible range of time and significance. A small word of great dichotomy, it slides down the continuum from its Latin root *momentum*, which merely means movement, all the way to a sense of influence and deep, moving power. Used lightly, *moment* can be an indefinite short space of time—an instant, a jiffy, a throwaway placeholder ("just a moment"). Or it can be fraught with importance, weight and gravity, as in "historic moment."

For Americans, 9/11 was such a moment. The horrific reality of the attack severed us into "before" and "after" attitudes about our country and our world. In the restless night following I remember waking up frequently and hearing my new mantra:

"Everything's changed." Blown away was our sense of safety and invulnerability; we lost our national innocence as one blow toppled two citadels of economic power in NYC, and another tore at the heart of military power in Washington, D.C. A momentous event, a never-to-be-forgotten date.

A moment of terror like 9/11 breaks with the past and portends a different future: we become aware of its formidable power to change our course and we recalibrate our vision to see new reality. One defining moment has brought each of us to an intersection in our lives and we must grapple not only with the enormity of the happening but also with its underlying influence on our future decisions. The fact that TV coverage enabled billions of people to share the same cataclysmic moment led us all to converge at the crossroads of past and future. A new paradigm was born.

For most of us, most of the time, moments of terror are comparatively rare. In our own personal lives we are more likely to have a moment of truth, an epiphany that visits us like a flash of light. In my life these moments of truth have mainly arisen in the simplest of exchanges. I recall such an unexpected moment in the midst of a brief conversation with my husband Bob when we were in our 40's. Bob had left Mother IBM and the "perks" of the corporate life to enter the brave new world of the entrepreneur. As the family money-manager of household expenses, I was accustomed to a degree of certainty concerning our cash flow, so I asked him what I thought was a reasonable question: "When do you think I'll be able to count on a regular paycheck?" His honest answer was, "Maybe never."

Out of all the myriad exchanges in our married life, why do I recall this one so clearly? Because it was a *moment.* In that particular instant, I understood—I "got" it. Something deep inside me said, "It is so." A fairly commonplace dialogue crystallized for me the indisputable fact that our partnership had sailed into uncharted waters. Yes, the process of change had been underway for months, but that moment with Bob coalesced my grasp of our situation; I realized that our "before" was ended and our "after" just beginning.

As Italian novelist Cesare Pavere once noted, "We do not remember days . . . we remember moments." A moment has an ephemeral quality and feels like a world unto itself. You can't force, predict, contain or package a moment. And only the lucky photographer succeeds in capturing that rare moment when the image melds the time, people and place to embrace the spirit of a person or occasion. Then the picture *is* worth a thousand words; it transcends the particular to portray the universal.

If you strung a bead for every joyous moment, what would your necklace comprise? Mine would have "inconsequential" moments like these:

a newborn baby gently sleeping in my arms during the wee hours of the morning
an unexpected call from a daughter who ends the conversation with "I love you"
a son's bear hug
a smile of recognition from an old friend
a comfortable silence shared
an insight grasped
a look of delight on the face of a grandchild
a flash of inspiration
a thoughtful gesture of caring
a spouse's delight in a longed-for achievement
an awesome glimpse of nature's beauty

Of course, like the Catholic rosary, our joyous beads are only one portion of our life's string. Joining the Joyful and Glorious mysteries are the Sorrowful. As we count these beads we are reminded how we ached for a suffering loved one, when tenderness turned into pain. We remember the moment when "cancer" was the doctor's diagnosis, and all else seemed to fade immediately into insignificance. Or when one small moment placed a barrier between a friend and one's self. Or when we *almost* understood a difficult concept, but it slipped from our brain never to return. Lost moments and troubled moments hang around our necks, too, whether we treasure them or not.

Carpe diem, goes the Latin phrase, "seize the day." But it may be more important to seize the moment. For Jesus, his "moment of truth" came during the temptations resisted during his 40 days in the wilderness. There it is reported in Luke 4:5, "And the devil took him up, and showed him all the kingdoms of the world in a moment of time." The vast panoramic array of history was offered as an enticement, a gift of authority and glory, but with a powerful "if"—*if* Jesus would worship the devil. And Jesus answered: "You shall worship the Lord your God, and him only shall you serve" (vs. 8).

Jesus met the critical moments of his life with unflinching resolve but he also strung the beads of many joyful moments as well. He was open to celebrations with friends, wedding receptions, dinners with tax collectors, encounters with strangers on the road. Moment by moment, we follow his pattern in our time here on earth, stringing our beads of joy and sorrow. The question is: can we recognize the numinous in the midst of the ordinary . . . the wise insight in a fleeting moment?

Moment by moment
We shape—
And are shaped by—
Our destiny.

Embracing the unexpected,
The inconsequential and insignificant,
The occasional "eureka" moment,
Those that define and bring truth
To ordinary life.

Gathering momentum,
We speed ahead,
Only to recognize later
The "aha" experience
In the midst of the ordinary.

Bless me with new vision, God,
That I may extract wisdom
From moments great and small,
And be transformed by them.

PAT

OF SOUND AND TOUCH

One day the very smallest of words (only three little letters!) clamored for my attention. I was called to respond to the insistent tapping of the word *tap*.

"Tap" and I have a special relationship; in my mind *tap* is permanently wedded with the word "dancing"—the joy of tap dancing, one of my earliest childhood memories. In the dance school I attended (and later, taught in) acrobatics and ballet were also favorite arts, but tap was by far the most *fun*! All those great staccato sounds coming from my *feet*! Add the delight of being in sync with the other tappers and, well, just the thought brings a smile to my face.

To this day, late in my life, an old melody once used as music for a dance routine will cause me to "tap" in my mind, replicating those old sounds and moves from my youth. Notice the phrase "in my mind": the patterns are indelibly etched but my feet no longer respond as quickly or agilely! So instead I revel in remembering the music and the patterns of movement, and celebrate that special section of my brain that preserves this remnant of joy from my youth. Like melodies rehearsed by singers, like much-practiced pieces by musicians, a dancer's brain embeds the steps of a bygone routine for a particular kind of instant recall. "On tap," so to speak, ready and waiting to be opened up by a song, evoked by a memory.

Originally, the noun *tap* meant a plug or stopper for closing an opening through which liquid is drawn. When used as a verb, *tap* transforms itself into an action word that penetrates, makes a hole, reaches into a given object or substance for the purpose of drawing off the contents within for use. Hence we tap our maple trees in the early spring, to draw off the sap, the essence of the tree's nurture, from deep within. A spate of sap may pour forth, but we all know how much distilling is required to net even a small amount of maple syrup. The raw material is far different from the final product. Yet God has great patience with the process. Nature teaches us by example.

From my childhood associations, tap is primarily an audible word, something you hear, a sound you make with your feet or fingers. But the sound is a by-product of another sense, that of touch: feet on floorboards, or fingers strumming on a table or door. Most taps are light touches, perhaps even timid or tentative in nature, certainly not demanding or assertive like another small rhyming word, "rap," which conveys a much harsher image. Something there is that is gentle about a tap, more akin to a whisper than a shout. Yet taps over time can take on an insistent quality that may be as imperative as a loud knock. Not unlike the incessant drip-drip-drip of a faucet, a persistent tap-tap-tap cannot be ignored.

To be tapped by someone is to be chosen for an honor or a responsibility: the tap starts the process, be it a new direction, office or position. It opens us up to new possibilities. In the 1960s I received one such tap from a Presbyterian minister zealous about liturgical reform; again, this tap involved dancing—but not *tap* dancing—this dancing was interpretive dancing used during worship. It was a radical idea at that time, disavowed by most traditional worshipers (and declared suspect by some even now). But, in parallel with his courageous decision to be in the forefront of the civil rights movement, the Rev. Wilbur O. Daniel simultaneously embraced liturgical renewal. So he tapped three women in his congregation to bring "a new thing" to the church services. He tapped us, and then got out of the way, demonstrating his faith that we would live up to his vision.

We were an unlikely trio: Juanita, Thelma and Evelyn. Unknown to each other, we were at-home mothers of young children. But Rev. Bill brought us together, and we began to originate a new worship form. Our dance workshops were replete with discussions of theology as well as choreography, as we sought to express the inexpressible for our worshiping community. Words, music and movement evolved into symbolic dance: a wholeness of mind, body and spirit synergized to worship God. We danced the poignant spiritual "Mary Had a Baby" at the Christmas Eve service, and moved many to tears. We created and presented three different versions of "The Lord's Prayer": one classic, one jazz, and one in the style of folk song (prayer will not be confined to only one expression!). Dubbed the "Spirit Dancers" by our pastor, we three danced in worship frequently until my move to Chicago converted the trio into a duet.

My body remembers these dance creations, and I can still "dance" them in my mind's eye. Liturgical dancing opened up new avenues of prayer, heartfelt insights, understandings of God; it played a great role in my spiritual formation in that decade. This is how God works: as we are creating and forming new vehicles for praise and adoration, God is making a new creation of us.

Not all tappings come from an external source, a person or a circumstance. Some tappings come from an inner, secret source, from the very taproot placed in us by God at our creation. In stillness and silence, we both hear and feel such tappings, muted or soft though they may be.

God taps us all the time, but we may choose not to hear it or to feel it as God's touch. As our years circle around, we become aware of a tap that has old echoes, a feeling of *deja vu*. That's because we've been tapped previously but have failed to answer the door; we have been called but somehow have not responded to the voice. Years later we may reflect on such a call—and see or hear it again for the first time.

Like those maple trees in the spring, we are tapped by God to bring forth our essence, our gifts to the world. And, as well as with the maple trees, God has great patience with us in this day-by-day process.

Are you paying attention to the secret taps of God, deep in your heart? Take time to listen, and respond. My hope is that, before taps is sounded to signal "lights out" to my time here on earth, I will have danced well, making pleasant sounds and pleasing patterns in my life and for others.

PAT

THE CUTTING EDGE

Do you remember that great feeling of invincibility in your youth? It was a "kissin' cousin" to the sense of immortality that rules us when we are young: we feel empowered to undertake all things, nothing is outside the realm of possibility, and death is some distant event that happens to other people. Such a philosophy of life gave rise to the old saying "Youth is wasted on the young." The reason it's wasted? Because they cannot conceive of *not* feeling the way they do: full of energy and aspiration, idealism and faith in their unlimited ability to overcome, hope in imagining a better way.

And it's normal and healthy for youngsters to approach life with such an attitude . . . but it's only a one-sided, partial view. It leaves out the shadow side of life. The unbounded optimism has yet to be tempered by the sharper edges of existence, the invincibility has yet to be tested. Their innocent spirits are not yet pierced by the realities of life that must be assimilated for wholeness.

The word *pierce* came to me one gray day in early December, not long after the anniversary date that still brings sadness after many long years, the date of losing our second child at birth. She was a girl, stillborn. No cries of life at delivery, only my own tears and wailing. A tearing, searing pain pierced my heart and rent my whole body. The ache was bottomless. Utter desolation after nine long, expectant months of gestation. All my high expectancy of the joy of giving birth came crashing down to deep despair. How could this have happened to me? To us? Still in our invincible, indomitable youth.

That was the day I count as my coming-of-age, my born-again day. The world wasn't perfect, and I was not all-powerful. Our loss was devastating, not to be believed. The usual denial: it must be a bad dream, a nightmare; I'll wake up and all this anguish will disappear. The bargaining: I'll do anything, God, just make it *not* so! The plea: spare me from this cruel reality. Don't dash away all our dreams for this new life, our first-born daughter. I really cannot stand the pain.

But it *was* so. The sudden, stabbing pain was real. The only question was: once pierced so deeply, how would I heal? Would the scar tissue of bitterness be the covering of my wound? Would there be "bad blood" stored somewhere in my unseen depths? How could I possibly walk into the light of a new day quoting St. Paul: "We know that in everything God works for good with those who love him, who are called according to his purpose" (Rom. 8:28)?

The truth is I couldn't. I would be dishonest if I claimed to have instantly made that great leap over the chasm of depression, to state that I was on my way to healing before the blood was dry. Instead I relied on the care, faith and love of others; I viscerally felt their prayers buoying my spirit, willing me to be able to deal with our loss. My mother-in-law offered her usual spirited support of our little family: my husband, our almost-two son, and me. Although wounded himself, my husband was the soul of compassion for me. Even our ever-busy toddler seemed to know that I needed lots of hugs and kisses and not too many demands; he was warm and visible proof that we could create a precious new life.

And then there was the intervention of unexpected "angels," strangers to our circle of family and friends. One in particular I will never forget, although I can't recall her name. She was a former missionary nurse, one of the staff members on the obstetrical floor of the hospital, and she realized the extent of my despair and loneliness when all the babies were wheeled by to their mothers. She said little, but she made it her habit to come in for a late-night cup of tea, when the other nurses took their break with each other. It was so much more than "tea and sympathy" she offered. Her quiet, steady and comforting presence brought me hope that I could survive this blow and remain positive in my outlook on life. I have no doubt that she was an emissary of heaven itself.

Slowly I realized that only a second piercing could thoroughly heal the first—to be pierced by God through the darkness so I could come into the light. The physical piercing had to be followed by a spiritual piercing, the second touch we must pray and hope for, even in the midst of our pain. Once pierced by the harshness of life we are never the same, but we must cling to the hope that God accompanies us in both the heights and the depths . . . perhaps, most especially in the depths.

I freely admit that being pierced is something I avoid. (I don't have pierced ears like most women I know—not to mention the piercing of other body parts that is prevalent today!) And the passion story of Jesus' piercing of his arms and feet before being lifted up on the cross is an image that cuts me deeply, as does the picture of his mother Mary watching his suffering that day (according to Luke 2:35, she had been warned by Simeon that "a sword will pierce through your own soul also"). But note how Jesus still communed with God, even in his ultimate hours of despair, asking forgiveness for others and addressing the Most High in his agony: "My God, my God, why have you forsaken me?" (Ps. 22:1a).

Like Jesus, people in pain need to lament, to vent their feelings . . . and to call on God to provide what is needed. Such help may come in the form of personal inner strength, a resolute spirit that we discover is far beyond our former ability to cope. Or it may emanate from external sources: people we love or even "angels unaware." In our distress we gratefully accept others, even strangers, as bearers of hope when we are hopeless. Being surrounded by the love and prayers of others facilitates the healing of our wounds. And always, we must remember to reach out and lift up our own prayers.

When I am pierced, Lord,
by lances that others throw,
by sharp words of criticism,
by the cutting edges of my life,
I bleed.

When the arrows of anger
are pointed at me,
are aimed at my heart
and perforate the mark,
I know pain.

When the vicissitudes of life
overtake me
and push me down
into the depths,
I anguish.

In all these circumstances
may the Holy Spirit come
to pierce me with love
and connect me with all creation,
I pray.

BARRICADE·BARRICADE·BARR
ICADE·BARRICADE·BARRICA
PAT

DE-FENSE! DE-FENSE!

One morning in the midst of peaceful meditation came a war-like word, one that I associate most strongly with a scene from *Les Miserables*. Can you visualize it with me? The French people, under siege, are heaping the street with barrels, timber, earth, carts, stones—anything portable, in truth, that will protect them from the royalist forces who are armed with real weapons and moving in to quell the uprising.

The word that created this image was *barricade*. From *barricata* (Italian) and *barricada* (Spanish), its origin is *barrica*, which means barrel, one of the common materials commandeered to throw up a hasty defense. Barricades are boundaries or borders, lines drawn to keep others at bay, forming a clear point of demarcation: "thus far, and no further" is the visual image given.

Viewed from the outside, a barricade is a barrier to keep others out, but we must also ask, "What is the barricade keeping *in*?" In the spiritual life this question shifts our probing to the defense mechanisms we each use to cloak our fears, to ignore real problems, to deny our uncertainties, to project our own shortcomings on others. Our many psychological ploys are adept at manning the barricades so that our usual comfortable mindsets remain undisturbed. For each of us it is much easier to call up our defenses than to risk being open and vulnerable as we reconsider old habits and set-in-stone automatic responses.

Some of my own defense mechanisms are like old buddies, comfortable companions that cycle in and out at crucial moments. If conflict arises, I tend to withdraw immediately behind my fantasy barricade of Wishful Thinking, where I hope that the situation will just go away. In the face of an unpleasant confrontation, I may well crouch behind my barricade of Stunned Silence. And, since I don't do Rage well, I may retreat to hide my Teary Sadness.

Over the years I have analyzed the building blocks of some of my barricades to discern which ones were worth keeping and which had to be dismantled. One of the barricades I chose to break down was named Self-Complacency. Ironically, this barricade was constructed from some really good stuff: a life generously showered with manifold blessings. But it had to go. It was keeping me from hard realities that burdened countless people in the community surrounding me. So I stepped over that barricade to enter into the suffering of others. In 1992, upon retirement from the business world, I committed to becoming a Stephen Minister, a compassionate listener willing to share the burdens of those who are trying to traverse a difficult life experience. This caregiving ministry brought me in daily contact with hurting people in severe circumstances: grieving the loss of a loved one, dealing with age and disability, coping with illness or divorce, or handling a sea-change in their lives.

Ostensibly, my motivation for joining this ministry was gratitude and compassion: gratitude for my own bountiful life, and compassion toward others who could be helped by a caring presence. At a deeper level, however, I suspect I was "righting the balance" of my own complacent, happy existence by subjecting myself to the tougher realities of life; I was tearing down a barricade that separated me from the possibility of my own wholeness.

And I have profited so much. I have witnessed the human spirit triumphing over the direst problems; I can testify that small miracles still happen. What began as loving service to others has flowed back to deepen and enrich me. I have experienced these words of Ralph Waldo Emerson: "It is one of the most beautiful compensations of this life that no man can sincerely try to help another without helping himself."

Many barricades cripple the possibility for fullness of life. Foremost are old wounds, be they unvisited, unforgiven or unhealed. The scar tissue becomes rigid and brittle; the person loses flexibility and malleability as response resources. Ensconced behind a barricade which shuts out the very person or action that could lead to renewed faith and hope and love, the wounded person has built a prison rather than a place of sanctuary.

Commonly, age has a way of erecting new barricades, of plastering on new layers of resistance to change. It's no wonder *Who Moved My Cheese?* has become a popular best-seller. It humorously captures this all-too-human attribute, this tendency to turn away from the new or unknown. I will be the first to admit that I am apt to choose the comfort of the known over the challenge of the unknown. To stay in a rut takes far less energy than to climb another mountain! Yet I assert this truth: when life has pushed me to the edges of discomfort, that is when my spirit has been stretched and when I have grown most in knowledge about myself.

Paradoxically, we cling to old patterns even though the pace of change around us quickens each day. We refuse to change even in micro ways, though we embrace the theory of evolution, which postulates that micro and macro change is built into the fabric of creation itself. Everyday realities teach us that nothing on earth stays the same. Take geography, for example. Our country's eastern coast is eroding, losing significant territory annually; when push comes to shove, old cartography must be abandoned for new. Scientific studies inform us that planet Earth is experiencing global warming; old assumptions about climate give way to new and probing questions about the ultimate effect of the glacial meltdown. Rain forests are being cut down at an alarming rate: how do we balance the needs of indigenous people with the destruction of the habitat of endangered species? And what untold resources are being destroyed before man can harvest them for good?

New questions of morality and ethics are battering away at barricades erected with old materials; the shifting sands of time force us to redraw our lines. I am reminded of a snippet of a verse from a favorite hymn, "Once to Every Man and Nation":

New occasions teach new duties,
Time makes ancient good uncouth,
They must upward still and onward,
Who would stay abreast of truth.

Examining our inner self is a front-line activity at the barricades we set up in our lives. In quizzing ourselves about deep-seated prejudices, in questioning our assumptions, in exposing our shadow side to the Light, we follow the pathway walked by Jesus Christ, who always pushed at the boundaries of his day's conventional wisdom. He would quote the accepted adage: "You have heard that it was said, 'You shall love your neighbor and hate your enemy'" (Matt. 5:43). But he wouldn't stop at the barricade, for he went on: "But I say to you, love your enemies and pray for those who persecute you" (Matt. 5:44).

Knowing my own limitations, and following Christ's example, I pray:

Teach me, God, to recognize my barricades to Your Spirit,
And to disassemble them:
Piece by piece,
Stone by stone,
That I may be permeable
To the loving wisdom
You choose to bestow.

PAT

THE BOTTOM LINE

The English language is a constant source of amazement to me. It sends me scurrying to the dictionary and other sources of etymology and quotations. And sometimes the smallest, most innocuous word can engender the greatest astonishment. Such a word was *net.*

Net, I thought, when it first arrived as a word-gift, it's a three-letter word that can catch butterflies and fish—and simultaneously point us toward the bottom line, not as in "seine" but as in "net profit."

The early disciples were mending their nets when Jesus called them from their vocation as fishermen to be fishers of people. Can you picture the ancient scene of this event? It was an ordinary day, and they were about a most ordinary task, maintaining the equipment of their trade. And then this charismatic rabbi called them to respond to a greater vocation, one full of risk and even loss, to follow a new way of life, to lead others in the spiritual journey.

And what was the *net,* the final result of their accession to Jesus' invitation to follow him? Merely a history-changing movement, a whole new faith growing out of the roots of Judaism.

Funny word, *net.* When it changes from its definition as a noun, "a woven fabric used to ensnare a creature" (or to keep creatures from feasting on us, as in "mosquito net"!) to an adjective (as in *net* result or *net* profit), it diverges completely and reveals its dual origin from two separate roots. As a noun *net* derives from *nett* in Anglo-Saxon and Teutonic usage and relates to sporting terms ("a bag or hook"), while its roots as an adjective are French, meaning "clear, neat, clean."

In the workplace I became well-acquainted with the adjective net—it's what most businesses are about: net profit, net results. In our company, which was predicated on consulting to the information technology arena, neither of these "bottom lines" was without great effort. To arrive at a net result was a daily process of information-gathering, number-crunching and painstaking analysis. The clients wanted a back-of-the-book answer from our technical reports and our staff of consultants: they literally thumbed through the detail and sought the pages containing certain end results. To our chagrin, many would rapidly bypass the technical and financial analysis to our conclusions, where they would exult, or despair, about their company's comparative ratings in the marketplace.

Underlying each net result is a process that has wound its way, labyrinth-like, through many steps to arrive at a central truth. Working through such a process as an individual is demanding enough, and I salute those who can persist with tenacity and patience to reach their final goal. But, even more, I reserve my unstinting admiration for people who facilitate groups toward decision-making; they display the ability to encourage a wide-ranging, honest discussion and then offer a few well-chosen words to sum up the result. Gifted facilitators can distill the woods of words into a concise statement of consensus. They instinctively know how to host a variety of opinions and yet achieve a net result.

In simpler times, the noun *net* conjured up an image of a person armed with a tool to catch butterflies or fish; both the net and its use were straightforward. But in our 21st century world, dominated by scientific progress and technical marvels, "net" has been co-opted as a short-cut handle for the Internet, which has forever altered our prior bucolic associations with the noun *net*. Today companies with vast and complicated networks trumpet the claim that "we're all connected."

But are we? Access to information and speedy electronic paths to it do not necessarily translate to our being more connected than ever before. Yes, communication is more pervasive, overwhelmingly so, and we are in a state of what some call "continuous partial attention" with multitudes of other people, but there are huge holes in our net of relationships. We communicate but do not commune, failing time and again to reach the stage of heart-to-heart intimacy.

As a facilitator of the spiritual life, Jesus communed; he was a master of the pithy phrase that people could store in their hearts. His aphorisms stand as singular examples of memorable net sayings. In his short ministry he probably preached daily, illuminating his disciples and the greater crowds surrounding him, yet comparatively few of his spoken words remain. In the gospel of John he left us with sweeping metaphors as net concepts: "I am . . . the good shepherd . . . the door of the sheep . . . the light of the world . . . the way, the truth, and the life . . . the vine, you are the branches."

Can you sum up the substance of your life so succinctly? In a retreat during my middle-years, the leader asked us to write an epitaph for our tombstone—an unsettling but rewarding exercise. In effect we were challenged to size up our net worth, not materially in what *we* possessed, but experientially, stating what kind of spirit possessed *us* and summed up our life. Truthfully, I don't remember the epitaph I wrote for myself at that time (no matter, it might be different today), but I do recall being shocked into a new awareness by the challenge it presented. Try it for yourself, and see.

Another exercise in taking the long view yet bringing your life into a net perspective is to write your own obituary (not as gruesome as it sounds!). You can craft your obit in the classical sense, listing primary relationships and various accomplishments during your lifetime. Or you can adopt the stance taken by the New York Times as they profiled the victims of 9/11 in their continuing coverage entitled "A Nation Challenged"—a more humanistic view that focused on what the dead had meant to others of significance in their lives, highlighting their *being* rather than their *doing*.

If an epitaph is too cryptic a medium for you, or an obituary too daunting, then choose a more expansive vehicle such as an ethical will. This term, "ethical will," was unknown to me until a fellow traveler on a tour to the Canadian Rockies introduced it. Our conversation came about in this way: I was endeavoring to describe the impetus and content of this book, then in progress. Her response to my faltering explanation was immediate: "Well, I think your writing sounds a lot like a Jewish document called an ethical will." Since I was uninformed of this tradition, she proceeded to explain that ethical wills spring from the belief that wisdom acquired during a lifetime should not die; rather, it is as much a part of a person's legacy as any material possessions. At the end of our short philosophical exchange, she promised to send me more information, and (blessings on her!) she did. Shortly after I returned home I received as a gift a helpful book entitled *So That Your Values Live On*, edited and annotated by Jack Reimer and Nathaniel Stampfer.

As I sampled the many examples of ethical wills in the above book, I felt confirmed in my own process. Yes, the judgment of my traveling friend was on target: this book of mine was closely related to an age-old tradition dating back to medieval and Renaissance times. And I was claiming my right, as a member of the older generation, to concretize my legacy in some tangible form. Though I hope my life has overtly modeled those precepts important to me, untold private motivations and deeper impulses have also shaped my choices. And I hope these less visible inner processes, revealed in this book, will be instructive to my children—and perhaps to other heirs in the Spirit.

In my spiritual journey I need occasions that thrust me out of the details of life into the stratum of net results. *Net* puts a period where before were only commas and semi-colons. *Net* captures an image and snares a concept. *Net* is the deftly-turned phrase with an enduring impact. *Net* is final, totally inclusive. *Net* is, for me, an unforgettable word-gift.

PAT

A LOFTY BREW

In my lexicon of word-gifts, I found only one that I failed to write about on the morning I received it. Time, ever the thief, must have robbed me of my journaling practice: the word stood alone, completely unexplored. Maybe it was too high for me to climb at that moment! The word was *steep*.

Steep is one of those words that can be either an adjective or a verb. The adjective *steep*, originally an Anglo-Saxon word, means precipitous, abrupt, lofty. The dictionary defines *steep* as having an almost vertical slope or pitch, a relatively high gradient relative to the area around it.

The relativity of *steep* caught my attention. On my ordinary walking route I feel I encounter some pretty steep hills (aerobically good for my heart!), and most of the time I huff and puff as I climb them, using all my go-power. Curiously, I notice when I am walking to get rid of pent-up frustration, my adrenalin powers me up those same hills with no huff-and-puff problem! In contrast to my experience while walking, however, these "steep" hills seem relatively tame in a car, as all six cylinders of the engine kick in to roll up the slope with ease. *Steep* is in the eye of the beholder—and the dynamic energy available.

Of the synonyms listed for the adjective *steep*, I liked the word "lofty." It evoked the deep spiritual response that mountains inspire in me. In my mind's eye I "see" the Grand Teton range in Wyoming, or the majestic Torres del Paine in Chile. Replicated in me is the same awesome response that ancient peoples felt about mountains, those steep places of mystery. Surely God's spirit is strong when we stand in the lofty places of this world.

And the mountains continue to attract sojourners and adventurers. Some tour the wonders of the old civilization established in Machu Picchu by the Incas centuries ago; others are magnetically drawn to the challenge of scaling Mt. Everest, despite the severe hardships and history of lives lost during such attempts. Their steepness is something to overcome for the beauty and triumph of arriving at the summit and surveying the incomparable scene viewed by so few.

Steep places figure prominently in the scriptures. In the Old Testament Noah's ark came to rest atop Mt. Ararat, and Moses journeyed up Mt. Sinai to receive the Ten Commandments from the Lord's hand. In the New Testament Jesus spoke with Elijah and Moses on a high mountain, was transfigured in the sight of his three closest disciples, and received God's benediction out of the cloud: "This is my beloved Son, in whom I am well pleased; listen to him" (Matt. 17:5).

Maybe it's the rarified air, but I find that being in the mountains renews my spirit. We commonly speak of "mountaintop experiences." Like the disciples of old, we often want to pitch our tents and stay there! But we know that we can't and won't: we must descend from the mountain and resume our ordinary life. At the end of a fruitful five-day retreat in the Sierras near Lake Tahoe, I reluctantly acknowledged that I needed to come to terms with this truth anew. In a small *lectio divina* group we considered Ex. 32:1-6 as our final passage before departure, and the phrase I chose was "come down from the mountain." As I meditated on this phrase, I began to write my own "commandments" on how to descend gracefully from this mountaintop experience and reenter life-as-usual. These were God's words to me:

1. Know that you have been on a high, so decompress slowly.
2. As you come down, do not descend too far into the valley.
3. Keep the image of the mountaintop in your spirit.
4. Give thanks for the experience.
5. Remember that I am everywhere, not just on the mountaintop.

Five commandments—only half of Moses' 10!—but words that I needed to engrave on my heart for a safe landing after being in steep places.

How do we overcome many of the "steep places" we find challenging us in our lives? My answer begins, strangely but not without relevance, with the image of millions of penguins nesting on an island in Antarctica. On the day I glimpsed such a sight, our boat was drawing close to the shores of South Georgia, which we approached by way of a U-shaped bay. An awesome spectacle greeted our eyes: black-and-white penguins, millions of them, perched from seaside to the very tops of the mountains. The appearance of such prolific life in the midst of a frozen landscape was breath-taking.

In Antarctica, the penguins that leave the icy waters early to breed obtain the best nesting places: those located not so far from the sea, the source of their food. Fiercely territorial, these early birds aggressively fight off any latecomers who want to stake their claim nearby; therefore the late arrivals must settle on nests progressively higher and higher on the knolls and hills. Eventually they entirely cover all available territory and blanket the island as if one organic, squawking and sprawling entity.

Now penguins are flightless. This means that the uphill settlers have the daunting task of hopping for miles downhill to the sea for food and then hopping miles uphill to regain their home nests and feed their chicks. Each small "hop" takes them closer to their objective, but it takes tremendous energy and an enormous number of hops to traverse the great distances.

This image of the penguin's plight relates to my own spiritual steep places. Much as I would like to solve many situations with a quick leap of faith or to fly away on wings of escapism, I know that like the penguins it's the hop, hop, hop of small steps that erodes the distance between the shores of my problems and the summit of their solutions. That's why most of the time I pray for strength for the journey—one hop at a time!

The verb side of *steep* is completely opposite in feeling. Unlike a steep climb, we are not asked to surmount or exert ourselves in any way; instead, *steep* invites us to be quiet, almost passive, to be still as our essence comes forth. This meaning of steep has its roots in Swedish (*stopa*) and Danish (*stoebe*), the practice of soaking barley for malting, in preparation for distilling a heady brew! The intent of this deep soaking is to soften, cleanse, or extract some constituent.

Doesn't this sound curiously akin to the spiritual discipline of contemplative prayer or meditation? In the spiritual life *steep* is closely related to the practice of abiding, just being with and dwelling with God. It conjures up a meditative exercise I once led, where I invited each person to imagine sitting at the bottom of a lake, immersed in the presence of God, allowing small bubbles of prayer to rise slowly to the surface. In the absence of any effort to move or swim, the group discovered that just settling in a deep place elicited wonderful insights, each bubbling up freely and freshly.

Steeping requires patience and time, like the brewing of a good cup of tea. A traditional tea-drinker, I spurn the method of quickly heating water in the microwave—a proper drink of tea is made with more deliberation and ceremony: place the tea or teabags in a warmed pot, cover with just boiling water, put a tea cozy atop . . . and then patiently wait for the flavor to develop.

When I steep in the presence of God, I turn off my sending transmitter and endeavor to become "all ears," an eager but passive receiver set. I settle down to await the spiritual soaking and to discover just what brew will emerge. The flavor of the experience varies, but not the disciplined practice. And this is what I have learned: in life we pay a steep price when we do not take time to steep.

PAT

GARDENING TIPS

One morning deep in winter I must have been unconsciously yearning for spring, for the word-gift that came was *bloom*.

My first and immediate association with *bloom* was a small sign in my office, a sign that I had carried from home to home, from state to state, in the early years of our marriage. Under our own volition we transplanted ourselves from our "just married" Virginia residence, where Bob served out his hitch in the army, to Massachusetts, where Bob enrolled in an MBA program at Babson College. When we ran out of money to continue schooling, Bob joined IBM ("I've Been Moved"), which transferred us in sequence to Minnesota, Illinois and New York, then back to Illinois for a second time before we settled in Connecticut for these past 30 years. During these wanderings I needed my small sign as a friendly prompt to my spirit: "Bloom Where You Are Planted."

You would suppose, with all the experience I had during those years of multiple moves, that I would have become proficient at the process. But I never did. Each move was a trauma, and each time for many months after our "transplant," I was too shocked to bloom in our new home.

Early on, the problem was resistance: I refused to put down roots. Our situation felt temporary and I chose to be detached. Growing roots takes energy and commitment, and in new environs I had little of the former and was chary with the latter. I didn't love where I was planted, you see, so I pretended to be just passing through. I would bloom next year, somewhere else, I told myself.

Fortunately, I learned from this early mistake. Tough as it might be to grow new roots, it was a far better option than to be rootless. So I purposely gave up feeling transitory and decided to work at blooming where I was planted.

For the truth was—and still is—that I do not transplant easily. It has always taken me considerable time and effort to put down new roots and learn to bloom in a new place. In contrast, other members of my family seemed to handle moves well: Bob embraced the challenges of a new position in the corporation, and the children soon found new friends and pursuits in the neighborhood. But I wilted.

Wilted at the sight of countless cartons to be unpacked . . . drooped at the onslaught of the myriad details and decisions necessary to set up our new domicile . . . withered as I faced the demands of establishing a whole new network of community associations and relationships. Most significantly, I keenly felt the loss of people left behind: I mourned all those everyday nurturing contacts that sustained me in the many avenues of my life.

Cultivating a place where you can bloom takes time and careful tending. No longer do I espouse the myth of rugged independence—experience has taught me how very much I need the gift of community. Cut off from familiar faces and places, I reevaluate all that I came to take for-granted in my old home: the comfort of driving "on automatic" to local stores rather than consulting a local map, street by street; the support of friendly neighbors who would be quick to offer assistance in an emergency; the assurance of ready and able health professionals who were intimately acquainted with our family; the confidence of relying on proven service outlets for car repair instead of unknown dealerships; the left-behind church that was "home" in every sense of the word, full of loving and caring friends.

Part of me understands and believes that with time I will flourish and bloom again in the new community; simultaneously, another part of me doubts that the blooming miracle will ever happen! My ambivalence sounds like the old scripture passage: "O God, I believe; help Thou my unbelief." Buoyed by my half-belief that it is possible to overcome the debilitating effects of being transplanted, I gradually relinquish my innate doubts and belatedly bloom again, reluctantly acceding that it is better to be a "late bloomer" than never opening up to new possibilities.

Perhaps if I were a gardener I would not only have more faith but also be more practical and realistic. But growing things is definitely not one of my talents. Our daughter Janet recognized my deficiency when she was merely ten: she laboriously crafted a thumb out of clay, painted it green, and presented it to me as a gift! (I still treasure my "green thumb" to this day.)

For me, gardening is like singing: I appreciate both talents but it's obvious I have little capacity for either. And I stand in awe of those who have the grower's gift. On the occasion of our 46th anniversary, a friend of mine named Sharon brought us an amazing and massive bouquet comprised of 46 various blooms from her garden—and she knew the Latin name for each! A most special gift from a most special person.

Not all blooms are tangible, readily apparent to our eyes and receptive to our touch. Some are invisible spiritual bouquets gathered by treasured friends who lift up prayers of hope for us during our hard passages of life. When our reservoirs run dry, they fetch the thirst-quenching water mentioned by Jesus (Matt. 25:35); they lend us their faith until we traverse the darkness and can once again respond like sunflowers, turning to the Light of God's love. Theirs are the most beautiful bouquets in the world.

In our extended family, one of the most memorable horticulturists was Bob's father, Ken, who practiced organic gardening before it became fashionable. Family lore gleefully reports anecdotes about his constant search for aged manure in local barns—and his counter-cultural uses of it, on his front lawn, for example. When he visited us at our first purchased home, situated in a suburban development in Illinois, he advised us to plant potatoes in the front yard as a prelude to tilling them under to create rich soil for what he assured us would be a *wonderful* lawn the following year. We knew he was agriculturally correct—but we opted for Scott's turf-builder products instead. Some blooms just aren't acceptable to suburban neighbors!

In our marriage partnership, Bob has always taken the lead as gardener: he has a knack for nurture, a passion for the process, a thumb that is definitely green. Apprenticeship with his father and his work as a kid on a local Massachusetts farm developed in Bob a "feel" for gardening, and for years he kept us knee-deep in blooms. He was noted for his dahlias, everything from huge dinner-plate specimens to smaller blossoms for flower arranging (my delight!). Year after year he planted hundreds of bulbs to bring spring joy. A recent Easter card could have been written for Bob: "Happiness is spring in bloom."

Even during our extremely "lean" economic times, as Bob's fledgling business struggled for survival, our home remained graced by flowers, inside and out. During those years we skimped on many optional purchases, but flowers were always on our "needed" list—it was our tacit, mutual agreement that we could not live by bread alone. We absolutely required the beauty of living plants around us. Knowing how we opted for such a frivolous extravagance in the midst of penny-pinching years has helped me understand the choices sometimes made by others who are strapped economically and yet splurge on a beautiful bauble rather than feed their physical needs.

Here in Connecticut, solidly planted in good soil for some 30 years now (many blooming cycles!), my feelings about the rigors of being transplanted still rise easily to agitate my heart. I remember my early days here, when the sight of a moving van was a dread apparition! Even this move "back east," which brought us closer to both sets of parents, set off in me the same cycle of bewilderment, the same sense of displacement, the same need to come to terms with a foreign terrain.

Eventually my transplanted self learned to bloom again, though I wouldn't want to repeat my 39th year, our first year here, which was excessively difficult. Our move to Connecticut converged with a significant passage in my life (reaching age 40!), when our children were growing more independent and I was deciding what our emptying nest might mean for the next chapter of my life. I recall how vigorously I resisted repeating the patterns that had come to dominate my 20s and 30s, even as I affirmed that those years had been full and fruitful. Motherhood and volunteerism were both worthy callings, but stirrings of "something new" provoked a restlessness of spirit. What new blooming was budding within?

Ultimately I felt called to reinvent myself for my 40's. I would bloom again, but I yearned for fresh fruits and uniquely new blossoms. A deep spading of my Connecticut garden brought me new roots of purpose, as I began to pursue an editorial career and later became a business partner with Bob. Life expanded as I made new connections within myself, developed latent skills and contributed to our children's college funds. Alongside this new venture I apportioned quality volunteer time to discover and celebrate kinship in the community. Neighboring blooms could not go unappreciated if we were to be a completely successful transplant in a new garden.

What circumstances encourage you to bloom? The list is tailor-made for each of us, I'm sure. Unique we each are, with a particular timetable that impels us to unfold. No forcing the bulbs to bloom when it comes to people! Like plants, we each need salutary conditions: arable soil, enough moisture, conducive temperatures, the right degree of light, careful tending. These external factors interact with our inner potentialities to create our chance to bloom, to contribute our essence to this world.

So this non-gardener, who hopes to bloom perennially at every stage of life, offers these spiritual gardening tips:

> Choose well your spot in the garden, and reach out
> to your blooming neighbors;
> Grow strong roots that can withstand periods of drought;
> Cultivate relationships that nourish and tend your
> spirit;
> Nurture the buds of potential within you;
> Secure enough Light for growth.
> And, finally, *Bloom where you are planted.*

PAT

HEAVY THINKING

Today has been set aside as a "writing day," an attempt to separate myself from usual pursuits and to be intentional about "unwrapping" one of my remaining word-gifts. So, before departing on a morning walk, I reviewed some word possibilities recorded in my old journals, hoping to prime the pump of my creativity. As I walked, I would "let go and let God" direct me to the appropriate word for today's literary efforts.

During the first mile my thoughts ranged widely over many areas but I purposely avoided consciously deciding on *the* word to wrestle with on this particular day—that was in God's hands. As I drew near to my outermost destination, the local pond and my meditation rock, *the* word had surfaced: *ponder* was the choice for today, the very word I had unconsciously been practicing on my meditative walk! What could be better than to ponder at the pond?

To ponder means, literally, "to weigh"; in French the root is *ponderer* and in Latin, *ponderare*. In the dictionary one of the first definitions is "to weigh carefully in the mind," and the adjective "ponderous" conveys the image of a formidable tome or a very large, slow-moving elephant. To ponder is to consider something deeply and thoughtfully, to meditate on serious themes or questions.

Some people are naturally bright and interactive, facile with words and comments, brilliant in repartee. That doesn't describe me! I seem to have an innate disposition inclined to pondering. But I had never connected *ponder* with weightiness. Yet, once revealed, the essential truth of that connection felt so right: To ponder is to consider weighty issues, ideas and decisions that are intrinsically important. Let "meandering" take care of the lighter stuff—pondering is profoundly suitable for heavy thinking!

When you ponder, you are casting about in a relative world, weighing current issues/ideas/problems against each other and against your inner standards/values/norms. You set up your own scales of justice as you weigh each side to determine validity and importance. Pondering is one pathway to seeking honesty and justice for your life.

In my journal I had written my own definition before consulting the dictionary, and I found some telling differences. I wrote "to ponder is to turn over in your mind and heart again and again." Furthermore, I needed God in the act: "to bring your thoughts and concerns before God for light and insight." These additions—"heart," "again and again" and "God"—are central to my own understanding of pondering, which must be heart-informed and not a mere exercise of the mind.

In the Bible we find the word *ponder* in Luke 2:19, the nativity story: "But Mary kept all these things, pondering them in her heart." A young and inexperienced new mother, Mary didn't know what to make of all the startling events surrounding her child's birth, so she suspended immediate judgment and pondered the significance of all those awesome happenings deep in her heart.

This biblical image of Mary I find very dear, and her response resonates with the experience of all parents, throughout all their children's years. You ponder as you feed your baby: how will I be a worthy mentor, a wise guide for this new little one? Or, later, when your child confronts you with an inexplicable act, you ponder how to avoid an irreparable breach while you negotiate between the wrongness of the action and the necessary consequences. No doubt Mary had many occasions to ponder as she watched her son be transformed from carpenter to Messiah and then witnessed his death on the cross.

Can you ponder without engaging the heart? Not in my view. If the heart is not actively engaged, what you term *pondering* may merely be analysis, the methodical sifting of information, where you separate entities into constituent parts and examine them critically to arrive at a conclusion. For sure, pondering is less precise, but more humble: it is living with the questions, not leaping nimbly to answers. Sometimes pondering leads to a decision, sometimes not; sometimes it only illuminates the edge of a problem, surrounding it like a nimbus but still leaving a darkened center. Still, the aura lingers to enlighten future meditations. And often in life we run into the "imponderables," those issues that cannot be explicitly explained or foreseen.

Introspection is not an unmitigated positive in my life. At times I must fight my innate disposition to ponder; I must instead decide to get off the merry-go-round. Somehow during the ride I have switched places: I no longer have a problem—the problem has me! Like a flawed CD I fall into a repetitive state of replay and fail to hit any new notes; I am caught in a pattern of frenzied circles as I tunnel through dark places. Then I need to let go of pondering (it is literally too heavy!) and put my energies into action.

There are times when quick decisions are imperative and pondering is out-of-the-question. Certainly when I was involved daily in the fast-paced business world, decisions had to be rapid-fire and immediate. But now my retirement stage of life generously allows for pondering time. Time for questions, and standing in-between the questions and elusive answers. And this "in-between" time is full of pondering, learning to love the questions themselves and embracing the process. Like a fluid ballet, those slow-moving turtle thoughts will eventually rise to the surface, given enough time; and elusive butterfly-insights will flit and glitter in tantalizing ways across the heart of one who waits. It seems akin to paying attention to the sacredness of the present moment.

It's possible that our ancestors, who performed more physical labor than is current in this high-technology age, may have had more time for pondering. After all, it is easier to bring your intent to focus on the everyday, sacred present when you are dedicated to manual labor or a repetitive task. Ironing is the modern-day bane of many women, and when I disclose that I actually like to iron, my friends shake their heads in disbelief! But I find it frees my spirit to let my hands go "on automatic" as I enjoy a rich time of rumination: plenty of undisturbed private time to chew and digest my own thoughts. These special moments are an opportunity to steep like a teabag and bring forth full-flavored reflections.

Of the synonyms listed for *ponder*—reflect, cogitate, deliberate, ruminate—the word "cogitate" caused me to chuckle as I recalled an incident at a NYC restaurant with our son Len and his wife Penny. We had finished our main course and our foreign-born waiter asked Len if he would like dessert. Stalling for time to make this momentous decision, Len smiled and answered the waiter's question by saying, "I'll have to cogitate." Imagine our glee when the waiter returned a few minutes later with an immense piece of *chocolate cake*—that's how he heard and translated "cogitate" into a dessert! We became helpless with laughter as Len stared at his unexpected treat—and of course he ate it all!

Although I failed to find "ponderings" (plural) in the dictionary, my friend Susan once wrote a column by that name in our monthly church newsletter. (When I informed her of this omission, she sparred: "We're not going to be limited by Webster, are we?") If she coined the title herself, it was aptly chosen; her words stood apart from all the narrative articles that reported ongoing events. In her column she elegantly captured the timeless essence of what was truly worth considering; her questions and observations encouraged the reader to begin pondering himself, and her invitation to join in the process of discernment was irresistible. By sharing her own ponderings she gave us permission to reconsider our blind spots and embrace God's vision.

On the way back home from my morning walk, I ran smack into a neighbor's blind spot. Busily watering some newly-strewn grass seed, he impatiently announced, "I want this to be grass *now*." Still deep in my pondering mode, I replied, "Some things just can't be rushed. It's nature's way." As I continued on, I reflected that this chance encounter and brief exchange perfectly summed up the word *ponder*: it can't be rushed because it takes time, quality time infused with heart and in sync with the creative process.

May your pondering moments be many, and your snap judgments few.

Jan. 1, What a morning, we got
went to the doctor and
and the wedding was lovely
we really
What if we never got

THE PRACTICE OF A WORD

During this writing project, *Webster's New Universal Unabridged Dictionary* has been a continual source of surprises. Several times I have turned to this large tome entirely confident that I already *knew* "my word's" definition and expecting a mere confirmation of meaning—only to be totally floored by the nuances and further ramifications offered by this official reference.

Such was my experience with the word *fuse*. Though I didn't have a clue as to why this word had been given, I was quite sure I knew what it meant, both as a noun and a verb. The verb *fuse*, I recorded that day in my journal, means to bring together, to unite, to connect into one. And the noun *fuse*, of which we have a boxful in the basement, is a safeguard, a device designed to protect our electrical circuits from being overloaded. Simple enough.

But what possible bearing could either of these disparate definitions have on my spiritual journey? The word *fuse* seemed far afield to my know-it-all self. A little humility brought me to the dictionary to be enlightened—and surprised.

The very first immediate realization reaped from the dictionary was that my view of those household basement fuses was limited: yes, fuses provide protection by melting the connection when the electrical wires become too hot—but this definition was only the benign aspect of the noun *fuse*. In less innocent circumstances, a *fuse* can be the means to *ignite* an explosion, sometimes with disastrous consequences. *Fuse* as a noun has a split personality, a real Dr. Jekyll and Mr. Hyde: Depending on its use and purpose, *fuse* can either protect or destroy.

Further perusal of etymology revealed that the word *fuse* has a complicated multiple parentage. Its Latin root *fundere* means "to pour" (I should have guessed that from my previous go-round with the word *suffuse*). But wait a minute. An earlier Latin root *fusus* means "spindle," which set me off on a completely different tangent of exploration.

As employed in earlier days of hand spinning, a spindle is a rounded rod, usually wooden and tapered at both ends, used to twist into thread the mass of fibers (raw materials like flax or wool) that are held by the distaff. From the jumble of raw materials the spinner seeks to extract a thread that is later woven into cloth.

So, I thought, *fuse* has a confusing mélange of meanings full of seeming contradictions: to pour and to unify, to create usable threads out of an unformed pile of raw stuff, to protect from system overload and to set off an explosion. The more I tapped into this word, the more I found myself confronted by a maze of possibilities but with no clear pathway as to its connection to my life. Feeling a bit dizzy from all the twists and turns it presented, I asked myself: "Where can I go to make sense of this word-gift?"

Suddenly my meandering thoughts came into sharp focus: *fuse* finally set off an inner light! The multi-faceted noun and verb of *fuse*—and the reason the word had surfaced for me in the first place—made perfect sense: it had to do with my practice of journaling. For years I have been pouring my thoughts into countless journals, daily writings that serve as the fail-safe, protective fuse of my life. Journaling is my way of unbottling emotions, of keeping my circuits from overloading. Nothing need be withheld in this safe and private space, and nothing is so helpful in keeping me from inappropriately "blowing a fuse" in my public life. In my journals I can set off explosions that will do no harm; instead, my private disclosures actually help me to pick my way through the minefields of human relationships.

Journaling for me is an avenue of prayer, another place where I meet God. Jesus assures us in John 14:2 that in his father's house there are many rooms; just as surely there are many pathways to that "house." As author Laurie Beth Jones writes: "I don't see prayer as being the act of beseeching so much as the acknowledgment of divine connection." In my journals, pen on paper, I make such a "divine connection." I enter new realms of possibility: a flood of words can carry away old grievances and soften any hardness of heart; one word at a time can start me on a book!

The phrase "pen on paper" in the paragraph above is the key to my romance with journaling. A pen in my hand viscerally connects my body, mind and spirit. It provides the magical link, a pipeline of sorts, to aid the flow of consciousness to find expression. The act of writing itself is therapeutic, as inner thoughts become visible to my own eyes through the medium of my own hands. I resonate with the observation of Cervantes, who called the pen "the tongue of the mind." Journaling is a silent practice that loosens my tongue and records words that otherwise would not be captured, and rarely (if ever) voiced.

Once I wrote a cinquain about this spiritual practice:

Journaling
Intimate scribblings
Remembering, Meditating, Reflecting
Words transforming, Creating life
Revelation.

The bottom line *is* revelation when I journal. All my life I have needed to write to make sense of my experiences; my journaling practice answers that old question, "How can I know what I think 'til I see what I say?" Others need to "talk it out," I know, but I have to talk to myself first by writing down words for my own eyes to see. Only then do I expose my feelings, analyze my motivations, untie knotty problems, ask myself penetrating questions. In rereading my old journals I recall events and emotions that, if unrecorded, I may well have forgotten. And, here and there, I pick up a thread that I have spun long ago and yet have not integrated into my story.

The Japanese talk about *shi-shosetsu*, the "I-story." That's their term for autobiography. In my journals there are bits and pieces of my "I-story" scattered throughout many pages: my "intimate scribblings" are like that mass of raw material sitting on the distaff, and I am attempting to spin these bits of memory into a cohesive whole. From my journals I cull meditative insights, take an honest look into the mirror of reflection, and fuse my stories of many years into a unity of one life lived—that's my ongoing process of liberation, discernment and integration.

When I open an old journal and reach back into the past, I encounter myself at another time and realize anew: we are surprises even to ourselves.

PAT

CENTERING

Every solstice during the year, and on other occasions as well, our church sanctuary is completely cleared of its seats and transformed into a welcoming space for a large 11-circuit canvas labyrinth. Similar in design to the ancient labyrinth of France's Chartres Cathedral, our local version was created during a two-week period in 1993. As part of this creative process, I was one of many people who knelt on the floor of a capacious local armory to assist in painting its winding pattern on the surface of the canvas.

People come from great distances to walk its pathway, those spirals that circle round and round, sometimes edging tantalizingly close to the center, only to spin out to the periphery once again. Those who participate in the meditative walk each have their own reasons—perhaps as many reasons as the number of people who walk it—but they share a common bond: each is a seeker in the spiritual life, an explorer trying to move closer to God. The labyrinth in its special way becomes a microcosm of their spiritual journey. Praying as they travel the loops, they hope to find the grace and peace of God as they reach the center.

Though I do not regularly walk the labyrinth (I become too distracted by the frequent passing of other walkers), one evening when I walked it early, before the crowds came, I discovered the numinous power of its central space. Like all powerful ecstatic experiences, it is hard to convey in words. In its center I felt totally quieted and keenly receptive, embraced by the Spirit and eternally connected to our Source. Spellbound, entranced by the mystery, I had to summon great willpower to rise and move out of the way so that others could be accommodated as they reached that center, a small patch of limited area.

Once you have drawn so close to the Presence and have been graced with an ecstatic moment, you cherish this divine glimmer as a precious gift of God's love. A kernel full of potential to bloom in the Spirit. When the word *kernel* was bestowed one morning in my meditation time, I relived my labyrinth experience and began to journal about another small but significant moment when God was so immanent.

That very first episode of feeling grace poured down occurred when I was nearing 13 years old. One Saturday afternoon, while walking from church to home after the sacrament of Confession (I was Catholic then), I was "surprised by joy," overcome by a deep and visceral "knowing," an inexpressible personal certainty of God's abiding presence. I was so startled that I literally began to leap with delight (a youthful response!). Such a burst of grace marked my spirit in an unforgettable way—that spot on a main avenue of my hometown, where God touched me and sowed a seed of joy, will forever be sacred in my memory.

A kernel is such a small thing; the word comes from the Anglo-Saxon *cyrnel*, meaning a little seed or grain. The dictionary first defines it as "the softer, edible part of a shell or nut"; then, moving from the organic to wider meanings, the dictionary expands to declare *kernel* as the central part of anything, the nucleus or core. How like my word-gifts: small, digestible pieces to ruminate on, a small grain given as bread for my spirit, propelling me closer to central truths and core values.

The organic nature of kernel intrigues me, because I prefer "organic people": that is, people whose behavior seems a natural extension of their true essence. Call me unsophisticated, but if I encounter a person full of pretensions, I immediately begin to flush with discomfort. An inner radar of intuition tells me that the posturing I see is not in sync with that person's inner core; the blips on the screen are erratic and give no true picture of her character. The precious spiritual kernel has been smothered by extraneous layers of a false persona. Inevitably I fail to navigate the labyrinthine pathway to her original center, and our relationship breaks down.

The labyrinth, with its spiraling twists and turns, is a comforting symbol for me. It reinforces my belief that there is no straight line to God—the spiritual pathway is most certainly *not* linear. Most folks trying to attain the spiritual mountaintop cannot assault it by climbing straight up! Rather, we circle round and round, revisiting the same views as we ascend, only to realize that the supposed "same view" may present a different perspective from the vantage point of various heights. And all the while we're climbing, hopefully drawing closer to God, we simultaneously approach some central truths about ourselves and our relation to this world. If we're open to expand our consciousness, we can appropriate tiny kernels of insight that may lead to wisdom.

On our journey God appears in many guises. And all our attempts at imagining God fall short—but imagine we must! Earlier in this book I suggested that God might be a Master Musician, directing the vibrating strings of the Universe. The idea has merit, but I also have imagined God as a Great

Magnet, a powerful lodestone; struck with this thought, I wrote: "Each of us is born with a small piece of your magnetism, which draws us to You as our lodestone." Many years later I read a story that resonated with this image of God in Rachel Naomi Remen's book, *My Grandfather's Blessings*, where she relates a 16th century Kabbalah myth about the cosmology of the world:

> In the beginning there is the Ein Sof, pure Being without manifestation, the Infinite, Absolute Source of the world. The world as we know it begins with the Or Ein Sof, an emanation of light from the Source. Rabbi Luria explains the fragmented nature of the world by postulating an accident of cosmic proportions: the vessel holding the Or Ein Sof shattered and broke open, and the light of God was scattered throughout the universe into an infinite number of holy sparks. These countless sparks of holiness are hidden deep in everyone and everything.

Isn't that a great story to live by? To recognize the divine spark in others, and to acknowledge our common origin. Is there any better way to imagine a beloved community?

A divine spark, a seed of an idea, a grain of truth, a kernel of wisdom—all related in God's cosmology, I'm sure. All proceeding from the Divine Source, gifts waiting to bloom, like the mustard seed Jesus lifted up in his parable in Matthew 13: 31-32, the smallest of all seeds but with the potentiality of becoming a hospitable tree for the kingdom of God. Or, in the language of the parable of the sower in that same chapter, Jesus invites us to be "good soil" for his seed-words, that we may bear fruit in this world and feed many.

What do I want to be when I grow up? The list is long . . . the goal still distant:

A person of radiant faith, a window letting in the light of God.

A woman without artifice, whose inner self is consonant with the outer projection seen by others.

A bringer of harmony, providing a bridge to understanding.

An appreciator and protector of this wondrous creation.

A font of compassion, overflowing to others.

An authentic writer.

A blessing.

All this I would be, from one small kernel. May God give the growth.

PAT

DON'T TELL MOM!

Don't tell Mom!

That's a phrase I often heard from our children when they were slowly but surely progressing from adolescence to young adulthood. Even now, when they choose to tease me, it's not uncommon to hear them banter in my presence, "Don't tell Mom"—even now, all three of them in their 40's, "the kids" still need their secrets.

As do we all.

Our children delighted in keeping their secrets from me, and that's how it should be. Secrets are essential in the development of the individual self, that first stage of awareness that separates the child from the parent. Swiss psychiatrist Dr. Paul Tournier says, in his book *Secrets*, "The right of secrecy is a fundamental prerogative of the individual." And he elaborates on how important secrets are to the essence of a person, especially as they mature.

Kids aren't the only ones to harbor secrets—adults have a penchant for secrets, too. The writing of this book was a secret closely held by me for a long time; it was too fragile an act of creativity to share until the manuscript was two-thirds completed. Even then it took tremendous courage to disclose my thoughts (and secrets!) to my husband Bob and two other trusted spiritual friends.

By now it's probably no secret that *secret* was one of my word-gifts. In French and Latin its root is *secretus*, past participle of *secernere*, which means "to separate." The noun *secret* is something done, made or conducted without the knowledge of others; the adjective *secret* means hidden, private, close-mouthed, confidential. A *secret* is a precious confidence hugged closely to oneself, a distinct piece of privacy separated from the known.

Upon graduation from college, I worked in a place where secrets both abounded and were vigilantly protected. The epitome of a hush-hush, super-secret governmental organization, the National Security Agency (NSA) was my first "real" job. NSA required all potential employees to undergo extensive background checks and a polygraph test to ascertain if you had any personal secrets that could make you vulnerable to being blackmailed by enemy agents. Hooked up to several electric connections, I faced my inquisitor (not too strong a word!), who began to pepper me with questions. *Loaded* questions.

Q: Are there any skeletons in your family closet?
R: None that I believed to be pertinent to being a technical writer.

Q: What opinion do you have of Communist China?
R: I think the rulers are probably not any worse for the average Chinese citizen than the Kuomintang regime had been. (I had just finished reading *China Shakes the World*, a discussion about the evolving Chinese society.)

Etc., etc., etc., until the final zinger:

Q: Do you realize you could jeopardize your husband's security clearance by your answers?

R: (Big jolt recorded on the polygraph, followed by nervous tears.) No reply.

Shaken to the core, I left the site of my polygraph test and paced unseeing through the National Gallery of Art as I awaited my husband's release from his duties that day. He greeted me with a cheery, "Well, did you pass your test?" Which of course started up my waterworks anew. Innocent though I was, I had been made to feel full of unacceptable secrets.

Today we realize that polygraph tests are a better measure of nervousness than a foolproof means of detecting secrets. But back in the 1950s, the heyday of McCarthyism, a mentality of suspicion ran rampant; everyone was a potential Red menace. Despite my obviously poor performance during the test, eventually I received my security clearance (the zealous inquisitor must have been overruled by cooler heads) and assumed my position as a technical writer.

In this rarified atmosphere of NSA's governmental secrets, I found it no challenge at all to be confidential about my low-level contributions to the cause, consigned as I was to writing operating manuals for early computers. In my sector of this bureaucratic maze, all work was carefully locked up each evening in "top-secret" files, and we were constantly cautioned to be completely close-mouthed about our particular projects and responsibilities. Keeping work-related secrets was easy. Later in my life, however, to be true to the secrets offered by friends was far more significant. And to accept that my children had secrets that they chose *not* to share was a far more difficult accommodation.

Secrecy is a close friend of mystery. Not just the "who-done-it" kind of mystery (though this genre thrives on secrets to keep us turning the pages), but the mystery inherent in the rites and practices of many religions. In Judaism, arcane and mystical teachings dominate the Kabbalah, which embraces the concept that some unknowns are meant to be beyond mortal reach: God's ways are unsearchable. In Catholicism, there is a "Secret" in the middle of the Mass! The celebrant pauses after the Offertory and before the Preface to whisper an inaudible prayer. Here, even in the midst of corporate worship, there is a special moment for the secret personal desires of the priest's heart. A secret in the most public of places, the church community—it seemed entirely fitting, somehow.

No one is without secrets, I believe, even in the closest of human relationships. It takes a lifetime to unearth our own secrets, to dredge them up from bits and pieces of memory or recollection, to expose them to the light. So, if we have secrets from ourselves, how can we not have secrets from each other? Our human covenant is this: I respect your mystery, and you respect mine.

Yet it is divulging those personal secrets to a trusted friend that leads to an unburdening and a greater clarity about who we are. In a person's development, says Dr. Tournier, keeping a secret is an early assertion of freedom; later, choosing to share your secret is important for a person's growth in openness and maturity.

To be chosen as someone's confidant is at once an enormous privilege and a serious responsibility. Accepting the disclosure of another person's secrets is an awesome sacred trust, one that I cannot undertake without a strong reliance on God and prayer. If we are humble in prayer, God shares the burden with us. God is our ultimate confidant, before whom we have no secrets: full disclosure is required. For in our heart of hearts we know the words of Psalm 139 are true:

Even before a word is on my tongue,
Lo, Lord, Thou knowest it altogether.

Jesus counsels intimacy with God in prayer and deplores the public spectacle of praying ostentatiously in the marketplace. In his prelude to the Lord's Prayer in Matt. 6:6, Jesus instructs his disciples:

> *But when you pray, go into your room and shut the door and pray to your Father who is in secret; and your Father who sees in secret will reward you.*

Therefore, in prayer we offer ourselves secretly and totally to our Creator:

> *Search me, O God, and know my heart!*
> *Try me and know my thoughts!*

For we want no separation in the form of secrets to come between ourselves and the Holy One; on the contrary, we seek to be transparent in God's presence, to be known just as we are, and yet also to be led by the power of the Holy Spirit to that which we *could* be. Let our prayer forever be: "Teach me wisdom in my secret heart."

PAT

LESSONS FROM A SPIDER WEB

Strand by strand, a spider carefully weaves its web. A marvel of design and complexity, the web stuns us with its perfection. Unexpectant, we come upon it in the garden one sunny morning; there it is, precariously strung between the branches of a low bush, glistening with dew. Whole and complete, though fragile, the web reveals the intricate pattern of the spider's work, captured for a moment in time. We stare in awe, transfixed by the spider's ability to weave something so beautiful out of a sticky substance from its own body.

The web reminds us: we too are weaving. Strand by strand during the moments of our life, through all the hours and days, the weeks and months, the seasons and years. Events become stories, stories become tales that verge on myth. A life builds, a web takes shape. But seldom do we take time to step back to view our creation, to seize a moment to grasp the entirety of our weaving: the singularity of one strand intersecting with another, its special and unique design.

Strand was one of my last word-gifts during this spiritually rich period of revelation in my meditative life. By the time *strand* appeared, I realized I had been weaving a narrative of remembrance, one word at a time. Meditation, revelation and reflection had zigzagged back and forth to create the web of my life in this book, which I began as a legacy for my children.

Do I believe that the strands of my life have been so special that recording them for posterity is merited? Not really. I readily admit that my passage here has been quite ordinary; many others have contributed more significantly to this world, thought more deeply, loved more radically and extravagantly. And, especially, others have written more eloquently.

But despite all these disclaimers, the fact remains that what I have woven is uniquely mine, like no other. And only I can disclose the "inside story," how the pattern developed through the decades of my time here on earth, and what intersections emerged as defining moments. Only by sharing can I give thanks for all I have been given.

Through the strands of our DNA heritage, the stuff of life itself, we are each handed the warp of our life, those threads set in vertical alignment, the unchangeable base we have to build on. We begin at our moment of birth to weave the weft, those horizontal threads that we shuttle back and forth on the loom of time. The weaving continues for a long time, if we are lucky, until the strands of the warp and the weft are so deeply intertwined that they can scarcely be separated from the pattern of the whole cloth, the fabric we have woven.

Since I am now past 70, I have already woven most of the cloth allotted to me! It has taken a lifetime to write this one book, this remembrance for my children and grandchildren. The urge to create this small legacy has lain dormant, much as the artist in Grandma Moses slumbered until old age, until the word-gifts from God encouraged the sleeping seeds to sprout into bloom. Perhaps it will afford my posterity a secret glimpse of my journey with God.

Now, from my "senior citizen" vantage point, I can take the "long view" of the strands of my life—my watch has been going on for more than three score and ten! As I stand back from the fabric in order to notice the patterns, I see differently with the spectacles of age. Some of the strands of my cloth jut out more starkly than others: the slubs of my missteps and other jagged moments contrast vividly with the smoother weave. Imperfections have been interwoven with the strong threads. Some areas draw the eye to dark spots of suffering, which I no longer ignore, for they taught me much I needed to learn: compassion, humility, acceptance and gratitude. The lows have been integrated with the highs of my experience. Only then is wholeness a possibility.

And just think! God, the Ultimate Weaver, sees all his weaver apprentices busily at work, so intent on their own lives that they often fail to realize that their little area of weaving intersects with so many others! In our self-absorbed busyness, we ignore the wise words of Chief Seattle:

All things are connected.
Whatever befalls the earth,
befalls the sons and daughters of the earth.
Man did not weave the web of life;
he is merely a strand in it.
Whatever he does to the web,
he does to himself.

Do we really feel this kind of universal connection? Even with the advent of the Internet and the ever-pervasive "web" that now dominates our lives, we cling to old images of being that solitary spider, whose handiwork has no connection with any other. God knows better. If only we could gain God's perspective.

Weaving is ancient,
An impulse felt by people long ago.
They wove tales around the campfires

Long before they interlaced strips of flax.
I wonder if they ever wondered
How we ourselves are interwoven?

We are not weaving in isolation: our strands touch, interlace, are interwoven with the lives of others. Two people join together to create a child, who comes forth with a unique strand of DNA belonging to no other. Created from a huge pool of possible chemical combinations supplied by the chromosomes carried in egg and sperm, a baby grows. Merely .1% of that child's genes conglomerate to distinguish him or her from any other human being. Each one of us is a miracle! We just fail to be awed by this basic fact of creation—birth is so ordinary, after all, an everyday occurrence. And we wrongly save the word "miracle" for other more uncommon events.

Woven together in the womb was this totally new creation, who joins a family . . . who joins a clan . . . who joins a community . . . who joins a nation, a world, a universe. The person looks solitary, seems individual and separate—yet written in his or her genetic code is a secret history, strands that connect that person back through countless generations. We each have a deep connection—indeed, a debt—to all who have ever participated in the process of creation.

Now some might say that in writing this book I have merely been "wool-gathering," grasping for threads and endeavoring to make a finished product out of disparate, unrelated episodes and events. Yet I say it has not just been indulgence in idle fancies and daydreams. No, I would use different analogies, "homemade" from my life:

- This book has been like a stockpot, long simmering in the kitchen of my soul, tended with patience and stirred 'round with love. The bits and pieces have been added over time to create what I hope is a tasty olio of flavors and a nourishing meal.

- Or, it has been like a long walk in the countryside to observe and enjoy the natural world. Some thoughts dart around like elusive butterflies, flitting from one place to another, and I run with my net to catch them. Other thoughts rise as slowly as turtles, surfacing rarely from the depths—I only hope that they are as long-lived as those creatures that lurk in the ponds and the seas. (Surely, these thoughts have been as *slow* in coming forth!)

And all these images—the stockpot simmering, the elusive butterflies, the slow-moving, ponderous turtles—have had to be laboriously interwoven in these pages. The "whole cloth" result is a medley of personal life experiences and observations, encounters within and encounters without, needing a lifetime to explore, blend and interact with each other to create something new, this personal recollection.

T.S. Eliot says it best:

And the end of all our exploring
Will be to arrive where we started
And to know the place for the first time.

This is the end, a full circle from the starting place, and I feel I have grasped all the strands for the first time. The word-gifts from God have been woven to create the tapestry of my life. Thanks be to God.

PAT

. . . AN OPEN ENDING

In ordinary life I seldom get "the last word." Others far more facile in conversation and skilled at repartee easily outstrip my ability to respond. Within the sphere of this book, however, this privilege has been granted to me—I *do* get the last word.

Given this rare opportunity, I had expected to be singularly delighted to reach the crucial step of penning the final chapter. Hadn't I always yearned to write one small, significant book? And, finally, after years of procrastination and attention to other priorities, hadn't I *almost* done it? Surely it was time to exult, to sprint down the track and joyfully break the tape at the finish line.

But instead of flexible tape, I ran smack into a stone wall of resistance, a wall built with conflicting and negative emotions. Full of angst, I experienced the quintessential writer's block. Rough draft after rough draft was attempted and then discarded. Nothing, but nothing I wrote did I deem eloquent enough to escape the trash basket. What inner turmoil was deterring me in my race to completion?

Topping the list of my unexpected emotions was an extreme reluctance to end my love affair with creative work: writing this book had become a way of life, and I was loath to let it go. In the chapter "Gardening Tips" I confessed that transitions are not easy for me, and that applies to endings as well, as revealed in "Saying Our Goodbyes." Obviously I was in conflict about relinquishing a process that had become so fulfilling for me.

This process—"unwrapping" word-gifts mysteriously bestowed one by one—I firmly believe was initiated by a Divine prompt. How else could this handful of ordinary words be chosen as gifts from the incredible richness of the English language? Why would *laughter* find its place among *sacred* and *deep*? How could *harmony* keep company with *asunder* and *pierce*? What could common words like *watch*, *narrow*, *departure* and *steep* offer in the spiritual life? And then there were those two three-letter words, *tap* and *net*—little powerhouses of exploration!

Perhaps the overall lesson here is to pay attention to God's daily communication and touch in the ordinary moments of our life. My everyday lessons have been many:

> That in my daily life it is wise to be *still* long enough for God to bestow a cosmic hug, to *suffuse* my body with loving energy.
>
> That in my schedule it is imperative to experience *fallow rest time* if I am to *survive* my challenges and have *balance* in my perspective.
>
> That I can *bloom* by climbing over a personal *barricade* or wrestling with a *secret*.
>
> That I can *ponder* with God all the issues in my heart, and God will help separate the wise *kernel* from the chaff.
>
> That God can *fuse* all the varied *strand*s of my life into a blessed *moment*.

What has resulted is this small book, in essence an extended essay of many chapters, ostensibly begun as a legacy for my children, but at some deeper level, written to illuminate me to myself! No wonder the words of Judith Guest, author of *Ordinary People*, resonated deeply within my psyche: " . . . writers do not write to *impart* knowledge to others; rather, they write to *inform* themselves."

Having been so richly informed by my word-gifts, my spirit clung to this creative process and refused to admit that, for an author, finality was a desirable objective! Despite all contrary arguments made in the heart of a reluctant writer, books are meant to be finished. Just as I had initially been called to write by the phenomenon of one-word-at-a-time, now an inner voice prompted me to pronounce this book complete, even though I had not "unwrapped" all my word-gifts. The process could go on, my writing could continue, my spirit could still aspire to grow—but this book was history!

Key to overcoming my reluctance to proceed was a moment of epiphany: it was *the book* I was finishing, not me or my life. For I know myself to be, in the words of Joan Anderson's book *A Year By the Sea*, an "unfinished woman." I am a work in progress! And so are you . . . and so is everyone. For each of us can understand the truth of an old poster that once decorated our teen-age son's (messy!) room: "Be patient . . . God isn't finished with me yet."

Originally, this chapter was entitled "Summing Up." It was a title that demanded finality, yet I was not feeling "finished." It felt as if I were putting a period (.) to my life, when I know that at most it's only a semi-colon (;), a punctuation mark indicating a separation between thoughts, a place to stop, to rest. It's impossible to "sum up" a life that is unfinished; some pieces of the puzzle are not yet put in place. And so this chapter has been renamed "An Open Ending." My words and the Word continue.

I would end with the words of an old hymn, words that best capture my hopes and dreams for this small work:

O, teach me, Lord, that I may teach
The precious things Thou dost impart.
And wing my words, that they may reach
The hidden depths of many a heart.

Amen.

ARTIST BIO

Pat Van de Graaf is an artist and printmaker. A long-time resident of New Canaan, she is an Artist Member of the Rowayton Art Center and an Artist Member of The Silvermine Guild of Artists. She is also a member of, and shows her work at, Print Studio South in Charleston, SC.

Pat has been printing for over 20 years and has studied at the Art Students League in NYC and Syracuse University. She graduated from the University of Bridgeport with a degree in Printmaking/Art History in the spring of 1990, having gone back to school as an adult student. She has also studied with the late printmaker Jim Egleson and with printmaker and former University of Bridgeport Professor Jack O'Hara.

Although she enjoys doing woodcuts and watercolors, she has concentrated on etching, sometimes combined with silk-screen techniques and hand-tinting, and has been experimenting with methods to achieve flat vivid color in combination with etching. This gives a more abstract quality to the print.

Pat's prints and paintings have won numerous awards in local and regional shows, and she is represented in various private and corporate collections.

In the majority of her work, design is key; Pat attempts to simplify the elements in the objects she sees, thus re-defining them so as to best convey their own special and unique beauty or directed emotion.

AUTHOR BIO

"A pen in my hand viscerally connects my body, mind and spirit." This self-understanding drew Evelyn J. Bergstrom to major in journalism at Douglass College (Rutgers University). Writing became the common thread in both her professional life and spiritual development.

Upon graduation from college Evelyn was employed by the National Security Agency as a technical writer of computer manuals. During the years when motherhood was her primary job, she opted to use her writing skills as a volunteer to produce newsletters, articles and other promotional materials for church and community organizations. Eventually she returned to the professional world to undertake a varied career that included editing a crossword puzzles magazine and preparing early childhood reading materials. At the end of her career she devoted 16 years to her husband's information services consulting firm, where she served as editor-in-chief and all-round administrator in charge of the company's infrastructure. She counts this partnership with her husband as a unique and rewarding adjunct to their marriage, now 50 years young.

In her personal life Evelyn adopted daily journaling as a prayerful way of seeking spiritual growth. For years she longed to write one small, significant book, one that would be a legacy for her children and for other heirs in the Spirit.

From her journaling she has produced *Inklings* as a thank-offering for all that has been given to her. In this meditative memoir she invites readers to ponder their own spiritual journeys as she reveals her own.

A faith tradition has always been an important part of Evelyn's life. She is an ordained elder of the First Presbyterian Church of New Canaan, where she also served as a deacon. In addition, she was part of the Leadership Team that brought to New Canaan the Stephen Ministry, a one-to-one caregiving ministry that companions people who are traversing difficult transitions in their lives; now, 12 years later, she still participates actively in that ministry.

A voracious reader, Evelyn can usually be found in the "religion and spirituality" section of bookstores — she is a self-confessed "book-a-holic." She feels that her reading and her ministries have united to form and inform her philosophy of life.

Evelyn and her husband Bob have three adult married children and seven grandchildren. After moving around the nation early in their marriage, they have been happily settled in New Canaan, CT for 33 years.

Printed in the United States
27446LVS00002B/5